PRIVACY
for Sale

PRIVACY
for Sale

How Big Brother and Others
Are Selling Your Private
Secrets for Profit

Michael E. Chesbro

PALADIN PRESS • BOULDER, COLORADO

For Joni, my heart and soul, my beloved,
and my best friend
And for Skye and Tommi, my buddies.

*Privacy for Sale: How Big Brother and Others
Are Selling Your Personal Secrets for Profit*
by Michael E. Chesbro

Copyright © 1999 by Michael E. Chesbro

ISBN 1-58160-033-X
Printed in the United States of America

Published by Paladin Press, a division of
Paladin Enterprises, Inc., P.O. Box 1307,
Boulder, Colorado 80306, USA.
(303) 443-7250

Direct inquiries and/or orders to the above address.

PALADIN, PALADIN PRESS, and the "horse head" design
are trademarks belonging to Paladin Enterprises and
registered in United States Patent and Trademark Office.

All rights reserved. Except for use in a review, no
portion of this book may be reproduced in any form
without the express written permission of the publisher.

Neither the author nor the publisher assumes
any responsibility for the use or misuse of
information contained in this book.

Visit our Web site at: www.paladin-press.com

Table of Contents

Introduction   1

Chapter 1:
Your Right of Privacy   5

Chapter 2:
Protecting the Privacy of Your Social Security Number   9

Chapter 3:
Protecting Your Credit Privacy   23

Chapter 4:
Protecting Your Financial Privacy   29

Chapter 5:
Protecting Your Medical Privacy   33

Chapter 6:
Protecting Your E-Mail Privacy   35

Chapter 7:
Protecting Disclosure of Your Information   45

Chapter 8:
Protecting Your Freedom of Information   49

Chapter 9:
Protecting Your Privacy in the Mail   61

Chapter 10:
Protecting Your Telephone Privacy   69

Chapter 11:
Protecting the Privacy of Your Home   75

Chapter 12:
Protecting Your Privacy in the Workplace   81

Chapter 13:
Protecting Your Privacy in the Military   85
Chapter 14:
Protecting Your Privacy When Confronted
by the Police   93
Chapter 15:
The Reality of Privacy Activism   99
Chapter 16:
15 Steps to Privacy   103
Appendix A:
Table of Cases, Laws, and Regulations Cited   107
Appendix B:
Privacy Information Resources   109
Appendix C:
Federal Legislation Relating to Privacy   113
Appendix D:
The Privacy Act of 1974 and
Amendments (as of January 2, 1991)   115
Appendix E:
The Video Privacy Protection Act
(Bork Bill) (as of April 1993)   161
Bibliography   167

WARNING

This book is written under the First Amendment right of freedom of speech, and although it contains various points of law it is *not intended as legal advice.* No book can provide legal advice for all circumstances. Laws may be changed, amended, or repealed over time, and may receive varying interpretations by courts in different jurisdictions. It is strongly recommended that you consult legal counsel regarding how any law or set of laws applies to your specific circumstance in your jurisdiction.

Neither the author nor publisher advocates that you violate any law or regulation to enhance your personal privacy. In fact, this book specifically recommends against violating the law as a means to enhance your personal privacy, because such activity tends to be counterproductive as a means of enhancing privacy and may result in increased scrutiny by various law enforcement and government administrative agencies.

Throughout this book there are mentioned various businesses, services, products, and resources, but mention does not constitute any specific endorsement of one or another. The author and publisher believe that the various businesses, services, products, and resources mentioned herein may enhance your personal privacy; however, there is no guarantee concerning their appropriateness to your specific situation. It is strongly recommended that you investigate any service, business, or the like before using it.

Neither the author nor publisher assumes any liability for your actions, gains, losses, or anything else that may happen to you as a result of using the information contained in this book. If some government agency sends its ninja-suited, jack-booted thugs to your house at 2 A.M. because you've dared question its need to track your every move from cradle to grave, you're on your own!

This book is intended *for academic study only.*

Introduction

This book reflects my personal experience with the invasion of privacy. This invasion is the result of an almost total disregard for privacy rights and freedoms by certain government agencies, businesses, and service organizations. Confronted with ever-increasing demands for more and more personal information, I began to question what possible need there could be for so many different government agencies, private businesses, and organizations to collect such large amounts of information about me:

"Fill out this form!"
"May I see your identification?"
"What's your Social Security number?"
"Where do you work?"
"What's your home telephone number?"
"What's your work telephone number?"

"Who's your supervisor?"
"What's your credit card number?"
"Papers, please!"

Now wait just a minute! Americans don't have to put up with these Gestapo-like tactics. We have Constitutional rights and freedoms, *don't we?*

What follows is my attempt to answer that question. The fact is that we do have rights and freedoms, and the right to privacy is one of them. However, our right to privacy continues to be sacrificed for one reason or another, with an almost complete disregard for the threats we face and the harm we suffer whenever our rights and freedoms are ignored.

Richard A. Spinello, the associate dean of faculties at Boston College, made an excellent observation in the January 4, 1997, issue of *America:*

> It seems quite evident that our right to informational privacy has been sacrificed for the sake of economic efficiency and other social objectives. As our personal information becomes tangled in the web of information technology, our control over how that data will be utilized and distributed is notably diminished. Our personal background and purchases are tracked by many companies that consider us prospects for their products or services; our financial profile and credit history is available to a plethora of "legitimate" users, and our medical records are more widely accessible than ever before. The net effect is that each of us can become an open book to anyone who wants to take the time to investigate our background.

It is my hope that readers of this book will come to

understand the threat to their rights, freedoms, and personal safety that can result from a disregard for privacy. By looking at the various laws and court rulings I hope to give those in a position to make and influence policy some idea of the importance of privacy in developing rules, regulations, and procedures. Furthermore, these laws and rulings should give the individual a basis to address his privacy concerns to those policy makers who are either unaware of (or choose to disregard) individual privacy rights and freedoms.

The information in this book is not intended as legal advice: every individual has the right to act on his own behalf in matters of law. This information may serve as a foundation for further study and for preparing yourself to demand and secure your privacy rights and freedoms protected under the law.

Chapter 1

▼

YOUR RIGHT OF PRIVACY

Black's Law Dictionary, 6th edition, defines the right of privacy as follows:

> The right to be let alone; the right of a person to be free from unwarranted publicity; and the right to live without unwarranted interference by the public in matters with which the public is not necessarily concerned. The term "right of privacy" is a generic term encompassing various rights recognized to be inherent in concept of ordained liberty, and such right prevents governmental interference in intimate personal relationships or activities; freedoms of an individual to make fundamental choices involving himself, his family, and his relationship with others.

The right of privacy is clearly recognized in federal law, as stated in Section 2 of Public Law 93-579 (5 U.S.C. Section 552a):

(a) The Congress finds that—
(1) the privacy of an individual is directly affected by the collection, maintenance, use, and dissemination of personal information by Federal agencies;
(2) the increasing use of computers and sophisticated information technology, while essential to the efficient operations of the Government, has greatly magnified the harm to individual privacy that can occur from any collection, maintenance, use, or dissemination of personal information;
(3) the opportunities for an individual to secure employment, insurance, and credit, and his right to due process, and other legal protections are endangered by the misuse of certain information systems;
(4) the right of privacy is a personal and fundamental right protected by the Constitution of the United States; and
(5) in order to protect the privacy of individuals identified in information systems maintained by Federal agencies, it is necessary and proper for the Congress to regulate the collection, maintenance, use, and dissemination of information by such agencies.

As we can see from paragraph (a)(4) of Section 2 of Public Law 93-579, "the right of privacy is a personal and fundamental right protected by the Constitution of the United States." This being the case, any rules or legislation that would abrogate our right to privacy cannot be allowed. In fact, the courts have stated that "where rights secured by

the Constitution are involved, there can be no rule making
or legislation which would abrogate them." (*Miranda v.
Arizona,* 384 U.S. 436, 491)

Speaking at the 166th Commencement at New York
University on May 14, 1998, concerning our right to privacy, Vice President Al Gore stated that

> Americans should have the right to choose
> whether their personal information is disclosed;
> they should have the right to know how, when,
> and how much of that information is being used;
> and they should have the right to see it them-
> selves, to know if it's accurate.

The Organization for Economic Cooperation and
Development (OECD), with its 29 member countries
(including the United States), stated in a news release in
Paris on March 27, 1997, that the "fundamental right of
individual privacy, including secrecy of communications
and protection of personal data, should be respected."

The right to privacy is not a new concept. It has been
recognized in U.S. law for more than 100 years. In fact, a
famous article published in the *Harvard Law Review* in
1890 stated in part that

> The intensity and complexity of life, atten-
> dant upon advancing civilization, have rendered
> necessary some retreat from the world, and man,
> under the refining influence of culture, has
> become more sensitive to publicity, so that soli-
> tude and privacy have become more essential to
> the individual; but modern enterprise and inven-
> tion have, through invasions upon his privacy,
> subjected him to mental pain and distress, far
> greater than could be inflicted by mere bodily

injury. (Samuel D. Warren and Louis D. Brandeis, "The Right to Privacy," 1890, 4 *Harvard Law Review* 193)

Even international law has recognized our basic right of privacy for many years, as stated in Article 12 of the Universal Declaration of Human Rights, adopted by the United Nations General Assembly on December 10, 1948.

No one shall be subjected to arbitrary interference with his privacy, family, home or correspondence, nor to attacks upon his honour and reputation. Everyone has the right to the protection of the law against such interference or attacks.

In considering the right of privacy the U.S. Supreme Court has repeatedly held this right to be so important that it is deemed to stem directly from the Bill of Rights as enumerated by the Constitution. State courts continue to recognize invasion of privacy as cause for civil action. We all have the right to be free from intrusion upon the solitude and seclusion of our private lives and personal information.

Although it would seem that the law and government policy are clear regarding protection of our personal privacy, our privacy rights and freedoms continue to be eroded as more and more agencies demand more and more personal information from us.

Chapter 2

▼

PROTECTING THE PRIVACY OF YOUR SOCIAL SECURITY NUMBER

One of the greatest threats to personal privacy is the unrestricted use of Social Security numbers (SSNs) as a national identification number.

In 1936, when SSNs were first issued, the federal government assured the public that use of the numbers would be limited to Social Security programs. Today, those assurances have come to mean nothing as the SSN has become a national identification number, resulting in a major threat to the privacy rights and freedoms of Americans everywhere.

Even as the idea of Social Security was being debated before Congress, there were men who recognized the threat to Americans that would result from the establishment of this type of program. Examples of comments by men of the day include these:

Never in the history of the world has any measure been brought here so insidiously designed as to prevent business recovery, to enslave workers, and to prevent any possibility of the employers providing work for the people. (Congressman John Taber of New York, April 19, 1935)

This bill opens the door and invites the entrance into the political field of a power so vast, so powerful as to threaten the integrity of our institutions and to pull the pillars of the temple down upon the heads of our descendants. (Congressman James W. Wadsworth of New York, April 19, 1935; taken from Arthur J. Altmeyer, *The Formative Years of Social Security*, 1966, 37–38)

Unfortunately, the fears and concerns of those opposed to the Social Security Act when it was proposed before Congress have come to pass. As the abuses of the SSN continued to grow, Congress attempted to correct this abuse by passing Public Law 93-579.

Section 7 of Public Law 93-579 (a)(1) provides that

It shall be unlawful for any Federal, State or local government agency to deny to any individual any right, benefit, or privilege provided by law because of such individual's refusal to disclose his Social Security account number.

Over and over the courts have held that Americans have a right to privacy and that common use of the SSN is a threat to that right. Examples of these holdings are the following:

The right of privacy is a personal right designed to protect persons from unwanted disclosure of personal information. (*CNA Financial*

Corporation v. Local 743, D.C., Ill., 1981, 515F, Supp. 942, Ill.)

The Privacy Act was enacted for the purpose of curtailing the expanding use of Social Security Numbers . . . and to eliminate the threat to individual privacy and confidentiality posed by common numerical identifiers. (*Doyle v. Wilson*, D.C., Del., 1982, 529G, Supp. 1343)

For example, armed with one's SSN, an unscrupulous individual could obtain a person's welfare benefits or Social Security benefits, order new checks at a new address on that person's checking account, obtain credit cards, or even obtain the person's paycheck. *** Succinctly stated, the harm that can be inflicted from the disclosure of an SSN to an unscrupulous individual is alarming and potentially financially ruinous. (*Greidinger v. Davis*, 988 F.2d 1344 [4th Cir. 1993], 1345–53.)

Furthermore, the courts held in *Yager v. Hackensack Water Co.*, 615 F. Supp. 1087, (D.C., N.J. 1985) that the Privacy Act applies to the private sector in the same way that it applies to federal agencies. Private agencies that request your SSN must comply with the provisions of the Privacy Act of 1974.

The U.S. Congress has frequently recognized the threat from unlimited use of the SSN as a common numerical identifier. Congressman Ron Paul of Texas introduced H.R. 3261, "The Privacy Protection Act," stating the following in his *Freedom Watch Newsletter* on April 29, 1998:

The expanding use of the Social Security

Number is a dangerous precedent with serious consequences for Americans everywhere. The number was originally used to administer Social Security benefits, but abuses of the number have grown and grown, effectively creating a national ID number that exposes innocent Americans to needless risk every day.

Using an SSN and one other piece of personal information, criminals can gain access to credit card files, bank accounts, and other information. Although eventually many of these scams are discovered and the victim cleared, a great deal of damage is often done in the process.

Congressman Paul continues:

> But the more important issue is one of constitutionality: the federal government simply does not have the authority to create this type of big-brother program. The question we need to be asking is this: Why does government feel like it needs to assign tracking numbers to Americans? Why does the federal government want to be able to track Americans from the cradle to the grave? This process is more indicative of fascist states, rather than societies which value individual liberty and privacy.

We are constantly warned of the dangers of disclosing our SSNs.

On February 27, 1991, Janlori Goldman and Lucas Guttentag of the American Civil Liberties Union (ACLU) made this statement before the House Committee on Ways and Means:

> Over the past 50 years, the SSN has evolved

from a single-use identifier to the identification number of choice for the public and private sector. It is possible to instantly exchange, compare, verify, and link information in separate databases, often without the knowledge and consent of the person divulging the information. Such a storehouse of information, inevitably made accessible to federal agencies, state governments, and private sector interests, presents a very real potential for abuse.

In its 1997 paper *Privacy in America: Social Security Numbers*, the ACLU stated:

> Because the SSN is so commonly used as an individual account number, this nine-digit code ends up being a virtual passkey to a vast amount of private, and often sensitive, information about you, your address, medical history, shopping preferences, household income, and use of prescription drugs, to name just a few.

In the March 1997 issue of *Black Enterprise*, J. Jerome Bullock, managing director of Decision Strategies International in Washington, D.C., wrote in the article "Protect Your Identity":

> Your Social Security number [and] your date of birth are the crown jewels of credit card fraud. . . . Question the need to reveal personal information, especially your Social Security number. When seeking general information, there is really no need for someone to have it.

The Federal Trade Commission (FTC) in its brochure

Identity Thieves Can Ruin Your Good Name, posted on the FTC Web site (http://www.ftc.gov/privacy/ updated May 20, 1998) advises:

> Before revealing personal identifying information, find out how it will be used and if it will be shared with others. Ask if you have a choice about the use of your information: Can you choose to have it kept confidential? . . . Give your Social Security number only when absolutely necessary. Ask to use other types of identifiers when possible.

Unrestricted use of your SSN as a common numerical identifier puts you at risk from criminals committing fraud, larceny, identity theft, stalking, and even murder.

On July 18, 1989, Robert John Bardo entered the apartment of Rebecca Schaeffer, the 21-year-old costar of the TV sitcom *My Sister Sam* and murdered her. In the months leading up to the murder, Bardo had obtained Schaeffer's SSN and other personal information and used his personal computer and a private investigator from out of state to stalk her. He had been able to pry into her personal life, learning her home address and many other aspects of her life she would have preferred to be kept private. As Bardo unlocked the secrets of Schaeffer's life, his obsession overwhelmed him. Finally, on a warm summer day in July, Bardo's obsession led to murder. This is obviously an extreme case, but nevertheless one that might have been prevented.

Identity theft is on the rise. Using personal information about you, such as your SSN and mother's maiden name, a criminal opens bank accounts in your name, obtains credit, and charges merchandise in your name. Of course, the criminal doesn't pay the bills, which are in your name, and doesn't care whether he bounces a few thousand dollars worth of checks, which are also in your name. He simply takes all he can get away with and leaves you trying to figure out what happened, explain it to the bill collectors, and repair your shattered credit rating. Eventually, such cases of identity theft are usually resolved and the victim cleared of any wrongdoing, but this may take months or even years to resolve.

No matter how long it takes, you will suffer some degree of financial damage and emotional stress and be forced to spend a significant amount of time trying to clear up the mess.

An article titled "Keep These Nine Digits to Yourself," in the August 1997 issue of *Kiplinger's Personal Finance Magazine,* recommends that you keep your SSN private to protect your financial security.

The August 1, 1997, issue of *Money* magazine in its article "Protect Your Privacy" recommends that you should never "disclose your Social Security number, your mother's maiden name, bank PIN number [sic], or e-mail password to anyone with whom you do not have an established relationship of trust."

In its Fact Sheet #14 called "Are You Being Stalked? Tips for Protection," the Privacy Rights Clearinghouse recommends the following:

> Be very protective of your Social Security number. It is the key to much of your personal information. Don't preprint the SSN on anything such as your checks. Only give it out if required to do so and ask why the requester needs it. The Social Security Administration may be willing to change your SSN. Contact the SSA for details.

Although the SSN was originally intended to be used only for Social Security purposes, its use was expanded in 1961 when the Internal Revenue Service (IRS) began to use it as a taxpayer's identification number. The Tax Reform Act of 1976 gave further authorization to use the SSN for other tax purposes, obtaining public assistance (welfare), obtaining a driver's license, and registering an automobile. No other use of your SSN is specifically authorized by law.

Although not specifically authorized, many other agencies, businesses, and organizations will ask for your SSN in the course of conducting business with you. In most cases none of these have a true need for it. It should not be necessary to disclose your SSN to cash a check at the bank, rent a video, obtain a library card, join a social club, donate blood, take a college course, or any of the other dozens of occasions when you may be asked to disclose your SSN. Remember, every time you disclose your SSN and it is recorded on some form or entered into some database, you risk having your personal information misused for criminal purposes.

One of the greatest condemnations of the widespread use of the SSN is that it is used for both identification and authentication. Some states use it as a driver's license number. Some businesses and even some financial institutions use SSNs as account numbers. Others use it to confirm your identity. At least one major bank identifies its customers by name and account number, but when called on the telephone asks the callers for their SSNs to confirm their identity. A company recently sent out credit cards to its customers. To activate their credit card customers had to call the company's automatic response system, enter their credit card number on a Touch-Tone telephone, and then enter their SSNs to confirm their identity and activate their card! The fact that your SSN is also part of your driver's license record at the department of motor vehicles (which in many states is a public record), is included in your account number at the local video rental store, and is perhaps posted on the student roster at the local community college completely defeats any effort to use it as a means of authentication.

Some agencies have cited Executive Order 9397, signed by President Franklin Roosevelt in 1943, as their authority to require disclosure of your SSN. In 1977, the Privacy Protection Study Commission recommended that EO9397 be revoked after some agencies had begun citing it as their authority to require disclosure of SSNs. Although EO9397 wasn't actually revoked, the Privacy Protection Study Commission's recommendation generally resulted in agencies' no longer claiming EO9397 as their sole authority to require disclosure of SSNs. (Once in a while you may still find some agency claiming EO9397 as authority to solicit your SSN, but it was never the intent of this executive order to provide a general authority for the unrestricted use of SSNs as a national identifier.)

Men and women serving in the armed forces face one of the most significant threats from the indiscriminate use of their SSNs. In the late 1960s the armed forces adopted the SSN as the personal identification number for each military member. This might be a reasonable use of the SSN (especially in regard to military pay and allowances), but in the military community SSNs are displayed with wanton disregard for the privacy rights of those men and women serving in defense of the nation.

The transient nature of military service (individuals are transferred to a new assignment and location every few years) puts military members at greater risk than their civilian counterparts from the unrestricted use of their SSNs. In the military environment, however, the SSN is displayed (and recorded) for almost everything a service member does.

In researching this book, I looked at the authority claimed by the military and its support agencies to require that service members disclose their SSNs for just about everything. Military support and services agencies generally cited 10 U.S.C. Section 3012 or 10 U.S.C. 8012 as author-

17

ity for requiring service members to disclose their SSNs. At other times they cited 10 U.S.C. 3013 and/or 8013.

In fact, these laws provided the military no authority to require SSNs; rather, they state the following:

> Title 10
> Section 3012. Department of the Army: seal
> The Secretary of the Army shall have a seal for the Department of the Army. The design of the seal must be approved by the President. Judicial notice shall be taken of the seal.
>
> Section 8012. Department of the Air Force: seal
> The Secretary of the Air Force shall have a seal for the Department of the Air Force. The design of the seal must be approved by the President. Judicial notice shall be taken of the seal.

Sections 3013 and 8013 define the duties of the secretary of the army and the secretary of the air force, but provide no specific authority to require SSNs or any exemption from the legal restrictions placed on the use of the SSN in other laws.

Each state also has its own version of a privacy act that generally follows the provisions of the federal Privacy Act of 1974. And remember that the courts held in *Yager v. Hackensack Water Co.*, 615 F. Supp. 1087, (D.C., N.J. 1985) that the Privacy Act applies to the private sector in the same way that it applies to federal agencies. Private agencies that request your SSN must comply with the provisions of the Privacy Act of 1974.

There are several things you can do to protect your privacy rights and freedoms when confronted with a request for your SSN.

- Adopt a policy of not disclosing your SSN unless specifically required to do so by law. If any agency insists on disclosure without providing specific legal authority to do so, protest this violation of your rights to the head of the agency. If the problem cannot be resolved, the law provides that you may file suit in district court for violation of your rights, and if the court finds that your rights were violated you will be awarded a minimum of $1,000.

- Determine whether disclosure of your SSN is specifically required by law.

- Ask for a copy of the Privacy Act. The law requires that each federal agency that maintains a system of records inform each individual it asks to supply information of the following:
   —the authority (whether granted by statute or by executive order of the president) that authorizes the solicitation of the information and whether disclosure of the information is mandatory or voluntary
   —the principal purpose or purposes for which the information is intended to be used
   —the routine uses that may be made of the information
   —the effects on the individual, if any, of not providing all or any part of the requested information

- It is your right to know under what authority anyone is requesting your private and personal information and what use will be made of that information once it is collected. If an agency cites a specific law or regulation as authority to obtain your SSN, ask to see (or research for yourself) the specific text of this law or regulation. Specific authority to require your SSN is very limited; however, many government agencies will cite some reference as their authority for requesting your information, which may or may not actually give authority for use of the SSN as an identifier in their records.

- Suggest reasonable alternatives to using your SSN. You will probably have to speak with a supervisor and explain the dangers of using your SSN as a common numerical identifier. Once confronted with a reasonable objection to disclosing your SSN, most quality businesses will gladly make other arrangements. If a business absolutely insists that you disclose your SSN as a condition of doing business, take your business elsewhere and recommend that others do likewise. There is almost no business requirement that justifies the risk of unrestricted use of your SSN.

- When dealing with schools you can cite a Supreme Court decision (*Plyler v. Doe,* 457 U.S. 202 [1982]) that held that requiring SSNs from all students would discriminate illegally against them. Furthermore, schools that receive federal funding must comply with the Family Educational Rights and Privacy Act (FERPA, also known as the Buckley Amendment, enacted in 1974, 20 U.S.C. 1232g) to retain their funding. One of FERPA's provisions requires written consent for the release of education records or personally identifiable information. The courts have stated that SSNs fall within this provision. If a school displays students' SSNs on identification cards, distributes class rosters or grade lists containing SSNs, or in any way makes students' SSNs available to others, it is a release of personally identifiable information, violating FERPA.

- Write to your elected representatives and ask that they introduce, cosponsor, support, and pass legislation that would prohibit use of the SSN as a common numerical identifier.

Although each official will have a specific address, you can send correspondence to the general addresses for the U.S. Senate, House of Representatives, and Supreme Court, and your letter will be delivered. The general addresses are as follows:

Members of the United States Senate
The Honorable (Full Name)
Senator from (State)
U.S. Senate
Washington, DC 20510

Members of the House of Representatives
The Honorable (Full Name)
Representative from (State)
U.S. House of Representatives
Washington, DC 20515

Members of the Supreme Court
The Honorable (Full Name)
(Title: Chief Justice or Associate Justice)
Supreme Court of the United States
Washington, DC 20543

Chapter 3

PROTECTING YOUR
CREDIT PRIVACY

Credit and credit cards are part of everyday life. In fact, it can be difficult to get along without a credit card in the modern business environment. If you attempt to make hotel reservations, rent an automobile, purchase airline tickets, establish an account at a video rental store, reserve seats at a concert, make dinner reservations at certain restaurants, or do any number of other things, you will be asked for a credit card number. In requesting a credit card number, the merchant is attempting to ensure that he will be able to recover his money if you fail to show up for or cancel your reservation or damage or fail to return some item that you rent.

When you charge a purchase to your credit card, it is recorded, and you are billed by your credit card company. This maks a permanent record (or at least a long-term record) of your purchase. Some credit card companies will provide you with a year-end summary of all your charges. All credit card companies maintain a record of your purchases to send with your bill and to resolve any dispute that may arise between you and a merchant or because of fraudulent use of your credit card.

When you present your credit card as payment for a purchase, the merchant makes an imprint of your card or swipes your card through a device that reads information from the magnetic strip on the back of your credit card and prints out a credit card receipt. The merchant then asks you to sign the receipt. The merchant retains a copy of the receipt and provides a copy to you.

From time to time, merchants may attempt to obtain additional information from you as part of the credit card transaction. This may include your address, telephone number, SSN, or driver's license number. The reason for this request is usually to obtain information for their mailing lists or future promotional advertising. Sometimes, however, the requests for additional information is not so innocent. An unscrupulous individual with access to your credit card number, SSN, and home address can cause considerable damage to your credit through fraudulent charges or other forms of identity theft.

Providing a merchant any information not recorded on your credit card is, from a privacy and financial security point of view, a very bad idea. All the major credit card companies, American Express, MasterCard, and VISA, have merchant policies that prohibit merchants from requesting any information not recorded on your credit card as part of the credit card transaction. Several states have also passed laws that prohibit merchants from recording information not on the credit card as part of a credit card transaction. For example, Section 1747.8 of the California Civil Code provides the following:

> Any person accepting a credit card in payment

for goods or services is prohibited from writing or recording the cardholder's personal information on any form associated with the credit card transaction. This includes but is not limited to address, telephone number, and SSN. The use of forms that contain preprinted spaces for personal information is prohibited.

Merchants can require that you show a California driver's license or ID card, or if not available, another form of photo ID. But this information cannot be written or recorded on any form associated with the credit card transaction. Violation of this prohibition is subject to a civil penalty of up to $250 for the first offense and up to $1000 for each subsequent offense.

Other state laws may be worded differently, but the idea is the same: A merchant may not record a cardholder's personal information as part of a credit card transaction.

In a letter dated May 22, 1998, Mary C. Schweitzer, director of administration and reporting for VISA International, emphasized the following:

> Please be assured that merchants may not refuse to honor a VISA card simply because the cardholder refuses a request for supplementary information. The only exception is when a VISA card is unsigned when presented. In this situation, a merchant must obtain authorization, review additional identification, and require the cardholder to sign the card before completing a transaction.
>
> Many cardholders have expressed concern about the recording of supplementary personal information on a bankcard sales draft. In

response, several states have passed legislation that prohibits requiring such information on the transaction form.

In a case where a merchant insists on recording your personal information as part of a credit card transaction, you should report this to the customer service departments of the credit card company in question, as well as to the Better Business Bureau and the state's attorney in states where the law specifically prohibits merchants from recording this information.

These are the customer service departments for the major credit cards:

American Express
Consumer Affairs Office
801 Pennsylvania Avenue, NW
Washington, DC 20004
Telephone: Call the number on the back of your
    specific American Express card.

MasterCard International
Customer Service
P.O. Box 28468
St. Louis, MO 63146

VISA U.S.A.
Customer Service
P.O. Box 649
Owings Mills, MD 21117-0649

In addition to being careful to not provide information that is not already recorded on the credit card itself, be sure to pay attention to what is recorded during the credit card transaction. Don't simply throw away your copy of the credit card receipt. Remember, your credit card number is record-ed on the receipt. In cases where a credit card transaction still uses carbon paper to make copies, be sure to take the carbons with you. (With the greater use of electronic transactions, car-bon paper is not as common as it once was, but this still may be used by some businesses.) Most stores don't shred their trash, so there is nothing to prevent someone from obtaining credit card numbers from a merchant's trash bin some night. Take a moment to look at the sales receipt itself; some sys-tems my record your credit card number on the receipt too.

As has already been mentioned, using a credit card pro-duces a specific record of your purchase. Therefore, it should go without saying that you should never use a cred-it card for any type of "sensitive purchase." If you don't want it recorded that you purchased a certain item, donat-ed money to a specific organization, or visited a particular place, don't use your credit card to conduct the transaction.

At least once a year, obtain a copy of your credit report from the major credit reporting agencies. This will allow you to review your credit report to ensure that information about your credit history is recorded accurately and that no one else's credit information has been posted to your file accidentally. Furthermore, it allows you to see who has inquired into your credit history because credit inquiries are recorded on your credit report. The three major credit reporting agencies are as follows:

Equifax
P.O. Box 740241
Atlanta, GA 30374

Experian (formerly TRW)
P.O. Box 2104
Allen, TX 75013

Trans Union
P.O. Box 390
Springfield, PA 19064

Another privacy concern associated with these credit reporting agencies is that they will provide information from your credit file to businesses seeking to offer preapproved credit to potential customers. If you have received preapproved credit offers in the mail, it is likely that one or more of the credit reporting agencies has released information about you to the business offering you credit. Some people may be interested in receiving preapproved credit offers, but generally I believe that preapproved credit is a bad idea for those of us seeking to maintain our privacy. If you seek credit with a business, it will make certain inquiries into your credit history, but you are aware of this when you apply. With preapproved credit offers you have no say about which businesses will inquire into your credit history.

Fortunately, each major credit reporting agency recognizes that preapproved credit offers may not be of interest to everyone. Each will allow you to opt out of preapproved credit offers. Contact the credit reporting agencies and ask that your name be removed from the lists they provide to companies offering preapproved credit to potential customers. This will not adversely affect your ability to receive credit. If you qualify for preapproved credit, you will qualify for credit that you apply for with the same business, but by restricting this personal information to those firms to which you specifically apply for credit, you control which businesses have the right to access information maintained by credit reporting agencies.

Chapter 4

PROTECTING YOUR FINANCIAL PRIVACY

How much money is in your checking or savings account? Where do you invest? What bank do you use? What did you purchase with last year's Christmas bonus? What's the limit on your credit card, and what credit cards do you use? How much did you receive in your last paycheck? How much did you pay in taxes last year?

All these questions seek to invade your financial privacy. Your personal finances should be private, but all too often there is little regard given to financial privacy by banks, credit unions, and other businesses. Call your bank, credit union, or credit card company and ask for some information about your account, such as the balance of your checking account or available credit on your credit card. After asking for your account number, the bank representative will likely ask for some piece of information to confirm your identity. Very often the information asked for is your

SSN and/or your mother's maiden name. We have already examined the problems involved with using your SSN as a means of identification or authentication.

Your mother's maiden name is a part of public record for anyone who cares to take the time to look. Records such as birth certificates, marriage licenses, and almost any record filed with a city or county clerk or in a court is available for public inspection.

Once the bank, credit card company, or other entity "confirms" your identity it will provide the information you have requested. It may also follow other instructions concerning your account, such as making payments or transfers. These things are done as a "service to the customer," and they do, in fact, make it convenient to conduct various financial transactions. The problem is that there is generally very little concern shown by these same institutions about protecting your privacy.

If someone writes you a check and you cash it at your bank, what information will the bank record on the check when you present it? One bank requires customers to endorse the check and record their account number, SSN, and telephone number on the back of the check. Another institution requires that you provide SSN, home address, home and work telephone, and place of employment. After the check clears, the person who wrote the check can request a copy of the canceled check from his own bank. Your bank account number, SSN, telephone number, and the name of your bank (from the cancellation/routing stamps) have now been provided to the person who originally wrote you the check!

Since 1970 the law has required that banks record both sides of all checks for more than $100. Sorting checks written for less than $100 from those written for more would result in an administrative nightmare, so banks simply record (microfiche) all checks they process. The bank therefore has a complete record of every business or person with whom you have dealt by using your checking account. Robert Ellis Smith, the editor of *Privacy Journal*, is quoted in the book *Bulletproof Privacy:*

> Your canceled checks record the names of your doctors and hospitals, the publications you read, the relatives you help, the religious and charitable activities you support, the volume of business you give your liquor store, and the amount you spend on transportation. The information in canceled checks can be a mirror of your life, a reflection that you do not want seen by the wrong set of eyes.

An article in the September 1997 issue of *Consumer Reports*, "Are You a Target for Identity Theft?", warns: "Retailers accepting your checks often try to write your credit-card, driver's license, phone, or Social Security number on the check to identify you. Tell them no (only a few states actually outlaw the practice) or pay with a national-brand check card, which debits your account for purchases without paper checks."

Of course, the most effective way of resolving the problems associated with checks is to not use checks. However, this may be a more drastic step than some are willing to take. Checks provide a convenient way of paying bills and sending money for other purposes through the mail. For routine uses it may be worth having a checking account. For any purchases that are not routine or are sensitive and for which you cannot pay cash, use postal money orders.

Black's Law Dictionary, 6th edition, describes a money order as "a type of negotiable draft issued by banks, post offices, telegraph companies, and express companies and used by the purchaser as a substitute for a check." The institution issuing the money order is directly obligated to accept and pay its money orders according to its terms.

The advantage of a money order is that it is not traceable by name to a specific individual. Money orders, once cashed, are recorded numerically. Thus, with your receipt it is possible to determine that money order PS123456789 was cashed by the XYZ Company, but it is not possible to find out what money orders John Smith submitted to the XYZ Company without knowing the money order serial numbers in advance or searching all processed money orders for information about John Smith.

Chapter 5

PROTECTING YOUR MEDICAL PRIVACY

We generally think of our medical records as private and conversations with our physician as privileged. Overall, this is true, but information about our health still may end up available to others without our knowledge or consent. Health-related questions are generally included in applications for life and health insurance. Information about claims filled for job-related illness or injury is on file. As is credit information, medical information is filed by a central bureau. About 10 percent of Americans have a file with the Medical Information Bureau (MIB). To find out whether you have an MIB file, write to the following address:

Medical Information Bureau
P.O. Box 105
Essex Station
Boston, MA 02112

If you have an MIB file, the agency will provide you with a copy of it, allow you to make corrections, and provide you with the name of anyone to whom your file has been released within the preceding six months.

For more information about the privacy of medical records, you can request a copy of *Is Your Health Information Confidential?* and *Your Health Information Belongs to You*, both available for a couple of dollars from the American Health Information Management Association.

> American Health Information Management
> Association
> 919 North Michigan Avenue, No. 1400
> Chicago, IL 60611

You can also contact the National Coalition for Patients Rights, which is dedicated to preserving the confidentiality of health care information.

> National Coalition for Patients Rights
> 405 Waltham, Suite 218
> Lexington, MA 02173

copy of your message on the backup tapes (copy number two). From the server your message is transmitted to your local Internet service provider (ISP), where it is forwarded to another domain and through other servers, all potentially making copies (copies three, four, five . . .).

Arriving at your friend's ISP, your message is put in a file where it sits waiting for your friend to log on and retrieve his e-mail. But your friend is out of town for a couple of days and doesn't log on to get his e-mail, so his ISP responsibly makes daily backups of its files (copies six, seven, eight . . .). Finally, logging in and getting his e-mail, your friend downloads your message to his incoming message file, where it is recorded on his computer's hard drive (copy nine). Now, assuming that both you and your friend securely erase the message from your own computers' files, there are still up to a half-dozen copies of your message recorded in various files and backup tapes.

There is very little to prevent the system administrator of any of these systems from reading your message.

You should view e-mail much like a postcard, where copies are potentially made of it at each post office along the way. There is, however, a simple way to prevent your e-mail from being read, no matter how many copies are made: use encryption in your e-mail communications.

There are several encryption programs available. For our purposes, we will look at a program called Pretty Good Privacy, or PGP. PGP was created by Phil Zimmermann in 1991 and has become the unofficial standard for secure e-mail since that time. PGP is available free for individual use on the Internet. Since 1991, there have been several upgrades to PGP, and improvements continue to be made.

I will not attempt to provide a PGP user guide here. There are several good PGP manuals available, and the help files that come with PGP provide easily understood instructions. Briefly, however, PGP uses a two-key method of encryption. When setting up PGP you create both a "public key" and a "secret key." The public key is used to encipher messages, and the secret key is used to decipher messages. You provide a copy of your PGP public key to anyone who might want to send you encrypted e-mail. Your PGP public key can be posted on your Web page and submitted to PGP key servers, where anyone who needs it can find a copy. Once a message is encrypted with your PGP public key, it can be decrypted only by using your PGP secret key. Even the person who encrypted the message with your PGP public key cannot decrypt it. Only your PGP secret key can decrypt a message encrypted with the corresponding public key, and, of course, you never provide your PGP secret key to anyone. It's secret!

PGP also provides you with the ability to digitally sign your messages so that the recipient can be assured that the message has not been tampered with. With a good PGP signature on the message, what was received is what you sent.

As an example of what an encrypted PGP message looks like, a previous paragraph has been encrypted using PGP.

hIwDyl3/dFcW8RkBA/9LkQmFBUztJLGi1zH
1U+rANeY59wdaNutxrVSaWiukF2Bj
AdfQYMuT/utXY+JPBW3mcjO+xO1VKQ1VB
VW+fWmvntV5tBXI/hA794fdXrLa1e/X
QGxxQVYrpRt96/Sq/SPjxdU17y4YnKyvVygd
tRQr6nC7jS+zI6KEfygM800Ri6YA
AAElmkR7WVXI5Xyr2PhrVguhlSnaOEao712J
DNaLqEX+2gGOQDWv46+6VaIPUzbJ
7F+A3Ui2+rR+fYQAKhE/kQ5IbOnFmN9I7do
wmMEkTIAK6i91tBi9gVlTD8X/Otl0
+QraMzaIL5v8jiim/eVN6Pc1bLcuPZBlrJj3cDq
ty7LcsmMD8nhg5wYIXFd13LEl
dzKOpkYN/wfG0QK14Xi5vBRL24+K30oxSL

N2KtAUea0P71l3xneQjVM1A+RSDZmD
Bf3MPKMigfyT+5o47g56PKE6SWd2XtBtZZA
HlvR4oBG644n0jmI7T3U2W+v8QeMw
2Iqbv9vPtHSqUakVpjiTOq9SCdNS/Xiz7XdG
EBBzSz7W6bXpEui7sBpwkqpwM/oV
RM6pb1TaoxA=
=N5TZ

I used an older version of PGP (Version 2.6.2) to encrypt the above message, since it is more commonly available than the new version 5.x. However, no matter which version you use, a PGP-encrypted message is unreadable. At the time of this writing PGP has not been broken, or at least no one has admitted to being able to do so. Given enough time, and with enough advances in technology, any encryption system can be broken. Yesterday's unbreakable cipher is today's example of the expertise of the code breakers. However, it may safely be said that PGP will provide you with a very high level of security for individual or business use. If you use e-mail and are concerned with your personal privacy rights and freedoms . . . get PGP!

Once PGP is set up on your computer, it is very easy to use. Encourage all your friends, associates, and business contacts (and anyone else with whom you communicate via e-mail) to get PGP and use it in any e-mail communications with you.

Now that you have PGP (or some other encryption program) for securing the content of your e-mail, you have solved part of your e-mail privacy problem. That is, although it may not now be possible to read the contents of your e-mail, it is still possible to keep track of whom you send messages to and whom you receive messages from. Not to despair, however; there is a way to give yourself a good deal of privacy in this regard.

Anonymous Remailers will take any properly formatted

e-mail message, remove the header (and thus the identifying information about the source of the message), and send the message on to a designated e-mail address.

At any given time there are several remailers up and running on the Internet. These remailers are run by groups or individuals in the interest of enhancing privacy in electronic communication. To find out what remailers are currently available, use a search engine and look for "remailer" on the Internet. Once you have found a list of current remailers, spend some time to learn how they work and practice using them. To get specific instructions for any given remailer, send a message to the remailer with the word "help" or "remailer-help" in the body of the text. The remailer should return an instruction file to your e-mail account. Basically, however, all remailers use the same general commands.

In addition to the "anon-to:" command, remailer commands include the following:

- *Latent-time*: This allows you to specify a delay for sending the message once it is received by the remailer. For example, "latent-time; +2:00" will delay your message for two hours after it is received by the remailer before it will be sent out.

- *Cutmarks* —: Any line containing only cutmarks -- and any lines thereafter will be removed from the message before it is sent. This allows removal of automatically appended signatures in some e-mail services.

- *Anon-post-to*: Allows anonymous posting to Usenet newsgroups.

- *Encrypted: PGP*: Many remailers have their own PGP keys. The "Encrypted: PGP" command allows you to send an encrypted message to the remailer. The remailer decrypts the message and then follows any instructions contained in the message as if it had received the message in plain text.

There are various other remailer commands that may be useful to you in your quest for personal privacy and freedom. You should request the help file from any remailers you intend to use and study them to take full advantage of a remailer's services.

There are a couple of advantages to sending your e-mail through anonymous remailers. First, of course, is that it allows you to send messages without disclosing your identity. Second, routing your e-mail through anonymous remailers hinders attempts at conducting traffic analysis of your e-mail. Since your e-mail is all sent through a remailer before being delivered, you have no direct e-mail connection with the person receiving your e-mail. The minor disadvantage of using remailers (at least type I remailers) is that they are a one-way gate. The person receiving your e-mail cannot reply by pressing an appropriate key or clicking on "Reply," but must compose a new message to respond to you.

As a brief example: To send an anonymous e-mail message you prepare your message using any common text editor. Whatever e-mail software you are using will probably work just fine. Now go to the first line of the body of your message and add two colons (::) to that line. The :: tells the remailer software that the next line is a remailer command. The next line of your message contains the command "anon-to:" and the address of the person to whom you wish to send anonymous e-mail. Skip one line and write the text of your message. The remailer will remove the message header and deliver the body of your message to the recipient anonymously.

For example, you would prepare your e-mail so that it looks like the following:

From: you@your email-address.com
To: remailer@remailer.com
Subject: ignore
::
Anon-to: receipient@his email-address.com

Here is some anonymous e-mail. Do you know who it's from?

The recipient receives a message that looks something like this:

From: anonymous@remailer.com
To: receipient@his email-address.com

Here is some anonymous e-mail. Do you know who it's from?

A remailer is only as secure as the administrator running the system: a systems administrator may be forced to disclose information from his system to law enforcement or other investigative personnel. However, remailers exist in different states and in different countries. It is a simple matter to chain remailers together so that a message is sent through remailers in several different states and countries before its being delivered to its intended recipient. When combined with PGP, remailers provide a very high level of privacy and security for your e-mail communications.

Remailers tend to come and go, depending on the interests and abilities of the people operating them. Also, there may be times when a reliable remailer is down for a brief period for maintenance or some other reason. For these reasons it is advisable to have a number of remailers to use. The following is a list of generally reliable remailers that were up and running during the time this book was being written:

Remailer	E-mail Address
redneck	config@redneck.efga.org
nym	config@nym.alias.net
squirrel	mix@squirrel.owl.de
bong	bongmailer@juno.com
wazoo	mix@wazoo.com
privacy	remailer@privacy.nb.ca
mix	mixmaster@remail.obscura.com
replay	remailer@replay.com
samson	remailer@samson.ml.org
lo14	remailer@lo14.wroc.pl
dongco	config@dongco.hyperreal.art.pl
cracker	remailer@anon.efga.org
neva	remailer@neva.org
hyper	mix@sind.hyperreal.art.pl
htp	mixer@htp.org

You can test these remailers by sending a message through them to yourself. (i.e., the "anon-to:" line should be your own e-mail address). The time it takes for a remailer to respond varies from just a few minutes to a couple of days. Some remailers also require that messages to them be PGP-encrypted. This is an added level of security put in place by the remailer operator. If you plan on using remailers, you will probably want to also use PGP in your e-mail communications.

Another step in maintaining the security of your e-mail is to establish e-mail accounts with the various free Web-based e-mail providers, such as Yahoo Mail, Hotmail, or Rocket Mail. If you have access to the Internet (such as at a public library, university, or Internet cafe), you can establish a password-protected e-mail account on the Internet. You simply go to the Web site of one of these providers, follow the sign-up instructions, and you have an instant e-mail account.

The service agreement with these Web-based e-mail accounts requires that you provide truthful information in the sign-up form, but the agreement does not require that you provide a specific address or any type of account information (the service is free, after all). Furthermore, these services do not attempt to verify any information you provide when you sign up.

Like the remailer services, Web-based e-mail providers are located in several different states and countries. This gives you the option of establishing several different accounts in many different locations.

There are several Web-based e-mail providers operating today. Some of these providers use programs such as NetScape to send and receive mail. Others provide special software to use their services, and some forward e-mail from their address to another e-mail address that you provide. To sign up for one of these e-mail accounts simply visit their Web site and follow the sign-up instructions. The following e-mail providers may be of interest:

Provider	E-mail Address
AkaMail	http://akamail.com/
Apex Mail	http://www.apexmail.com/
Bigfoot	http://www.bigfoot.com/
CMPnet Mail	www.cmpnetmail.com/member/login.page
Hotmail	http://www.hotmail.com/
Juno	http://www.juno.com/
Lycos Mail	lycosemail.com/member/login.page
Mail Excite	http://www.mailexcite.com/
Net@ddress	http://netaddress.usa.net/tpl/Door/Login?
NetForward	http://www.netforward.com/
Rocket Mail	http://www.rocketmail.com/
Web Email	http://wwdg.com/email/
Yahoo Mail	http://www.yahoo.com/

Chapter 7

PROTECTING DISCLOSURE OF YOUR INFORMATION

Once a government agency or other institution has obtained information about you, there is only so much that you can do to prevent disclosure of that information. There is a law that governs disclosure of personal information maintained by government agencies and, to a lesser extent, a law governing records in the private sector. However, even when dealing with government agencies, you cannot be sure that your personal information is being properly protected. Bureaucracy, lack of understanding by clerks and various other government employees, or simply a general disregard for the law and the rights of individual citizens by these same employees can lead to the unauthorized disclosure and misuse of your personal information. Most of us recall the scandal reported in the press a few years ago involving IRS employees who were checking out the financial status of their favorite stars without any official authorization.

Likewise, there is little to prevent your neighbor, say, who works as a teller at your bank from checking out your bank records. Someone interested in finding out who your friends and business associates are may have a contact in the telephone company's billing office who may be persuaded to provide information from your telephone records. The file manager in your employer's personnel section may be convinced to release information from your personnel file.

To help prevent such disclosure of your private information, you must make it a point to ensure that any agency or business with which you deal is aware that you are concerned about personal privacy and that you do not consent to any disclosure of information the firm maintains about you without your written consent. If you become aware of situations where agencies or businesses are acting in a way that could lead to the disclosure of personal or private information (e.g., requesting unnecessary information as a matter of policy or throwing away papers containing personal information without first shredding them), address your concerns to the agency heads or business managers and request that they change their policy. In cases where you see a total disregard for your privacy rights and freedoms, file formal letters of complaint, contact regulatory agencies, and, if necessary, file suit in the courts to protect your rights and recover any damages you may suffer.

When dealing with agencies or businesses about your personal privacy rights and freedoms, it is usually a good idea to provide them with the law or laws that apply. Concerning disclosure of information by federal agencies, you can cite the Privacy Act; when dealing with state agencies or businesses, there are state privacy acts and laws and regulations governing business conduct.

The Privacy Act (5 U.S.C. Section 552a) provides that "no agency shall disclose any record which is contained in a system of records by any means of communication to any person, or to another agency, except pursuant to a written request by, or with the prior written consent of, the individual to whom the record pertains." The act further states that "the term *record* means any item, collection, or grouping of information about an individual that is maintained by an agency, including, but not limited to, his education, financial transactions, medical history, and criminal or employment history and that contains his name, or identifying number, symbol, or other identifying particular assigned to the individual, such as a finger or voice print or a photograph . . ."

Furthermore, the act provides that "each agency that maintains a system of records shall establish appropriate administrative, technical, and physical safeguards to insure the security and confidentially of records and to protect against any anticipated threats or hazards to their security or integrity which could result in substantial harm, embarrassment, inconvenience, or unfairness to any individual on whom information is maintained . . ."

We saw that the courts held in *Yager v. Hackensack Water Co.,* 615 F. Supp. 1087, (D.C., N.J. 1985) that the Privacy Act applies to the private sector in the same way that it applies to federal agencies. However, too often private agencies and businesses are unaware of the provisions of the Privacy Act or the fact that the courts have held that it applies to them. Even when you are dealing with federal agencies whose employees should be aware of the provisions of the Privacy Act, bureaucracy often overrides law and common sense.

When dealing with any government agency, be sure that its representatives understand that you do **not** consent to the disclosure of your personal information to any other person or agency. If an agency does, in fact, release information about you without your permission, or if it has a policy of doing so, you must protest this clear disregard of your rights and freedoms.

Provide the agency with a copy of the law and insist that it change its unlawful policy. Very often, government agencies collect or disseminate information as a matter of "policy" or in accordance with their "standard operating procedures." However, no agency may lawfully establish policy or procedures that violate the law.

Remember, with regard to privacy the U.S. Congress has found that "the right of privacy is a personal and fundamental right protected by the Constitution of the United States." Further, regarding rights protected by the Constitution, the courts have stated: "Where rights secured by the Constitution are involved, there can be no rule making or legislation which would abrogate them."

Chapter 8

▼

PROTECTING YOUR FREEDOM OF INFORMATION

The Freedom of Information Act (FOIA) (5 U.S.C. Section 552) was enacted to provide the general public with access to federal government records. The basic idea of the FOIA is that a well-informed general public will enhance the accountability of government agencies. This type of openness is most beneficial for our constitutional form of government.

Although the FOIA only applies directly to federal agencies and records, all 50 states have also passed their own version of the act.

Once a federal agency has received your FOIA request, it has 10 business days to respond to you, stating whether it intends to comply with your request or deny it. If the agency denies your request, you may appeal the decision.

The agency then has 20 business days after receiving your appeal to respond with a decision regarding your appeal. If the agency denies your appeal, and you still want to obtain access to the records, you must bring your case before a federal district court.

There are some categories of information that are specifically excluded from disclosure under the FOIA. These categories apply to information that fit the following definitions:

(1) (A) specifically authorized under criteria established by an executive order to be kept secret in the interest of national defense or foreign policy and (B) are in fact properly classified pursuant to such executive order;

(2) related solely to the internal personnel rules and practices of an agency;

(3) specifically exempted from disclosure by statute, provided that such statute (A) requires that the matters be withheld from the public in such a manner as to leave no discretion on the issue or (B) establishes particular criteria for withholding or refers to particular types of matters to be withheld;

(4) trade secrets and commercial or financial information obtained from a person and privileged or confidential;

(5) intra-agency or interagency memorandums or letters that would not be available by law to a party other than an agency in litigation with the agency;

(6) personnel and medical files and similar files the disclosure of which would constitute a clearly unwarranted invasion of personal privacy;

(7) records or information compiled for law enforcement purposes, but only to the extent that the production of such law enforcement records or information (A) could reasonably be expected to interfere with enforcement proceedings, (B)

would deprive a person of a right to a fair trial or an impartial adjudication, (C) could reasonably be expected to constitute an unwarranted invasion of personal privacy, (D) could reasonably be expected to disclose the identity of a confidential source, including a state, local, or foreign agency or authority or any private institution which furnished information on a confidential basis, and, in the case of a record or information compiled by criminal law enforcement authority in the course of a criminal investigation or by an agency conducting a lawful national security intelligence investigation, information furnished by a confidential source, (E) would disclose techniques and procedures for law enforcement investigations or prosecutions, or would disclose guidelines for law enforcement investigations or prosecutions if such disclosure could reasonably be expected to risk circumvention of the law, or (F) could reasonably be expected to endanger the life or physical safety of any individual;

(8) contained in or related to examination, operating, or condition reports prepared by, on behalf of, or for the use of an agency responsible for the regulation or supervision of financial institutions; or

(9) geological and geophysical information and data, including maps, concerning wells.

Concerning these exemptions, however, the law provides that "any reasonably segregable portion of a record shall be provided to any person requesting such record after deletion of the portions which are exempt under this subsection."

If the federal agency states that it will comply with your request, it will assemble the information requested and make it available to you. Depending on what information you have requested, it may take some time to compile the records. The time limits cited above only require the federal agency to make a decision concerning your request. It will probably take most federal agencies some time to actually fill your request.

When making an FOIA request it pays to be patient, though persistent. Your request should be as detailed as possible to enable the federal agency to locate the information you are seeking.

The sample FOIA request letter on page 53 will help you in submitting a request for information.

Both the president and the attorney general of the United States have recognized the importance of freedom of information within the government. The memorandum from the president on page 54 and the attorney general on pages 55–56 were sent to all agency heads to show current directives regarding the FOIA.

Date

Your Name
Address
City, State, Zip Code

Head of Agency or FOIA Manager
Agency Name
Address
City, State, Zip Code

Re: Freedom of Information Act Request

Dear Sir or Madam:

In accordance with the provisions of the Freedom of Information Act (5 U.S.C. Section 552), I request that you provide me with copies of the following records: (clearly identify the records you wish to obtain)

I am requesting this information for the following purpose: (state the reason for your request)

If there are any fees for researching this information or copying the records I have requested, please inform me prior to acting on this request.

As you may be aware, the FOIA permits you to waive fees when the release of the information is considered as "primarily benefiting the public." I believe that my request clearly falls within the category of benefiting the public and is not in my commercial interest. Therefore, I ask that you waive any associated fees.

If all or any of this request is denied, I request that you cite the specific exemption that you believe justifies this denial and inform me of the appeal procedures available to me under the law.

I would be most grateful if you could handle this request as quickly as possible, and I look forward to your reply within the next 10 days as required by law.

Thank you in advance for your prompt response and attention to this important matter.

Sincerely,

Signature

Contact: The White House, Office of the Press Secretary

October 4, 1993

MEMORANDUM FOR HEADS OF DEPARTMENTS AND AGENCIES
 SUBJECT: The Freedom of Information Act

I am writing to call your attention to a subject that is of great importance
to the American public and to all Federal departments and agencies—the
administration of the Freedom of Information Act, as amended (the
"Act"). The Act is a vital part of the participatory system of government.
I am committed to enhancing its effectiveness in my Administration.
For more than a quarter century now, the Freedom of Information Act
has played a unique role in strengthening our democratic form of government. The statute was enacted based upon the fundamental principle
that an informed citizenry is essential to the democratic process and that
the more the American people know about their government the better
they will be governed. Openness in government is essential to accountability and the Act has become an integral part of that process.
The Freedom of Information Act, moreover, has been one of the primary
means by which members of the public inform themselves about their
government. As Vice President Gore made clear in the National
Performance Review, the American people are the Federal Government's
customers. Federal departments and agencies should handle requests for
information in a customer-friendly manner. The use of the Act by ordinary citizens is not complicated, nor should it be. The existence of
unnecessary bureaucratic hurdles has no place in its implementation.
I therefore call upon all Federal departments and agencies to renew their
commitment to the Freedom of Information Act, to its underlying principles of government openness, and to its sound administration. This is an
appropriate time for all agencies to take a fresh look at their administration of the Act, to reduce backlogs of Freedom of Information Act
requests, and to conform agency practice to the new litigation guidance
issued by the Attorney General, which is attached.
Further, I remind agencies that our commitment to openness requires
more than merely responding to requests from the public. Each agency
has a responsibility to distribute information on its own initiative, and to
enhance public access through the use of electronic information systems.
Taking these steps will ensure compliance with both the letter and spirit
of the Act.

(s) William J. Clinton

MEMORANDUM FOR HEADS OF DEPARTMENTS AND AGENCIES
Subject: The Freedom of Information Act

President Clinton has asked each Federal department and agency to take steps to ensure it is in compliance with both the letter and the spirit of the Freedom of Information Act (FOIA), 5 U.S.C. 552. The Department of Justice is fully committed to this directive and stands ready to assist all agencies as we implement this new policy.

First and foremost, we must ensure that the principle of openness in government is applied in each and every disclosure and nondisclosure decision that is required under the Act. Therefore, I hereby rescind the Department of Justice's 1981 guidelines for the defense of agency action in Freedom of Information Act litigation. The Department will no longer defend an agency's withholding of information merely because there is a "substantial legal basis" for doing so. Rather, in determining whether or not to defend a nondisclosure decision, we will apply a presumption of disclosure.

To be sure, the Act accommodates, through its exemption structure, the countervailing interests that can exist in both disclosure and nondisclosure of government information. Yet while the Act's exceptions are designed to guard against harm to governmental and private interests, I firmly believe that these exemptions are best applied with specific reference to such harm, and only after consideration of the reasonably expected consequences of disclosure in each particular case.

In short, it shall be the policy of the U.S. Department of Justice to defend the assertion of a FOIA exemption only in those cases where the agency reasonably foresees that disclosure would be harmful to an interest protected by that exemption. Where an item of information might technically or arguably fall within an exemption, it ought not to be withheld from a FOIA requester unless it need be.

It is my belief that this change in policy serves the public interest by achieving the Act's primary objective—maximum responsible disclosure of government information—while preserving essential confidentiality. Accordingly, I strongly encourage your FOIA officers to make "discretionary disclosures" whenever possible under the Act. Such disclosures are possible under a number of FOIA exemptions, especially when only a governmental interest would be affected. The exemptions and opportunities for "discretionary disclosures" are discussed in the Discretionary Disclosure and Waiver section of the "Justice Department Guide to the Freedom of Information Act." As that discussion points out, agencies can make discretionary FOIA disclosures as a matter of good public policy without concern for future "waiver consequences" for similar information. Such disclosures can also readily satisfy an agency's "reasonable segregation" obligation under the Act in connection with marginally exempt information, see 5 U.S.C. 552(b), and can lessen an agency's administrative burden at all levels of the administrative process and in litigation. I note that this policy is not intended to create any substantive or procedural rights enforceable at law.

In connection with the repeal of the 1981 guidelines, I am requesting that the Assistant Attorneys General for the Department's Civil and Tax Divisions, as well as the United States Attorneys, undertake a review of the merits of all pending FOIA cases handled by them, according to the standards set forth above. The Department's litigating attorneys will strive to work closely with your general counsels and their litigation staffs to implement this new policy on a case-by-case basis. The Department's office of Information and Privacy can also be called upon for assistance in this process, as well as for policy guidance to agency FOIA officers.

In addition, at the Department of Justice we are undertaking a complete review and revision of our regulations implementing the FOIA, all related regulations pertaining to the Privacy Act of 1974, 5 U.S.C. 552a, as well as the Department's disclosure policies generally. We are also planning to conduct a Department-wide "FOIA Form Review." Envisioned is a comprehensive review of all standard FOIA forms and correspondence utilized by the Justice Department's various components. These items will be reviewed for their correctness, completeness, consistency, and particularly for their use of clear language. As we conduct this review, we will be especially mindful that FOIA requesters are users of a government service, participants in an administrative process, and constituents of our democratic society. I encourage you to do likewise at your departments and agencies.

Finally, I would like to take this opportunity to raise with you the long-standing problem of administrative backlogs under the Freedom of Information Act. Many Federal departments and agencies are often unable to meet the Act's ten-day time limit for processing FOIA requests, and some agencies—especially those dealing with high-volume demands for particularly sensitive records—maintain large FOIA backlogs greatly exceeding the mandated time period. The reasons for this may vary, but principally it appears to be a problem of too few resources in the face of too heavy a workload. This is a serious problem—one of growing concern and frustration to both FOIA requesters and Congress, and to agency FOIA officers as well.

It is my hope that we can work constructively together, with Congress and the FOIA-requester community, to reduce backlogs during the coming year. To ensure that we have a clear and current understanding of the situation, I am requesting that each of you send to the Department's Office of Information and Privacy a copy of your agency's Annual FOIA Report to Congress for 1992. Please include with this report a letter describing the extent of any present FOIA backlog, FOIA staffing difficulties and any other observations in this regard that you believe would be helpful.

In closing, I want to reemphasize the importance of our cooperative efforts in this area. The American public's understanding of the workings of its government is a cornerstone of our democracy. The Department of Justice stands prepared to assist all federal agencies as we make government throughout the executive branch more open, more responsive, and more accountable.

—/s/ Janet Reno

Which government agencies are likely to have information about you in their files? The answer to this question depends largely on what, if any, interaction you have had with government agencies. Have you ever served in the military? Have you ever held a security clearance? Have you ever been investigated or convicted of a crime? The majority of Americans do not have records about them maintained by the government, but there are several million (both living and dead) who do.

Here are some agencies to check with about government files on you:

Federal Bureau of Investigation
Freedom of Information Privacy Section
935 Pennsylvania Avenue, NW
Washington, DC 20535
(Records of criminal investigations, et al.)

Defense Security Service
Office of Freedom of Information Act (FOIA)
    and Privacy
1340 Braddock Place
Alexandria, VA 22134
(Records of security clearance background
    investigations)

National Personnel Records Center
9700 Page Boulevard
St. Louis, MO 63132
(Records of personnel discharged from
    military service)

Too often, law-abiding citizens are confronted with requests for personal information by government agencies with little or no clear and specific explanation why this information is needed and exactly how it will be used. There is a law to protect our right to know what information is being collected about us, why it is needed, and how it will be used.

Public Law 93-579 states in part:

> The purpose of this Act is to provide certain safeguards for an individual against an invasion of personal privacy by requiring Federal agencies, except as otherwise provided by law, to—
>
> (1) permit an individual to determine what records pertaining to him are collected, maintained, used, or disseminated by such agencies;
>
> (2) permit an individual to prevent records pertaining to him obtained by such agencies for a particular purpose from being used or made available for another purpose without his consent;
>
> (3) permit an individual to gain access to information pertaining to him in Federal agency records, to have a copy made of all or any portion thereof, and to correct or amend such records.

One way to respond when confronted with a request for information by a government agency is to request that it also provide you with detailed information about its request. Before providing information to an agent of the government, present him with a "Public Servant's Questionnaire" and request that the agency answer the questions therein to enable you to determine your rights and obligations to provide the information being requested of you. The idea for the Public Servant's Questionnaire came from Lynn Johnston, author of *Who's Afraid of the IRS?*.

PUBLIC SERVANT'S QUESTIONNAIRE

Public Law 93-579 states in part that

> The purpose of this Act is to provide certain safeguards for an individual against an invasion of personal privacy by requiring Federal agencies to—
> (1) permit an individual to determine what records pertaining to him are collected, maintained, used, or disseminated by such agencies;
> (2) permit an individual to prevent records pertaining to him obtained by such agencies for a particular purpose from being used or made available for another purpose without his consent;
> (3) permit an individual to gain access to information pertaining to him in Federal agency records, to have a copy made of all or any portion thereof, and to correct or amend such records . . .

The following questions are based on the provisions of Public Law 93-579 and are necessary to make a reasonable determination regarding my disclosing personal information to you and your agency.

1. Name of Agent: _____
2. Residence Address: _____ City: _____
   State: _____ ZIP: _____
3. Name of Agency Requesting Information: _____
4. Agency Address: _____ ____ City: _____
   State: _____ ZIP: _____
5. Supervisor's Name: _____
   Telephone Number: _____
6. Agent's Proof of ID: (ID number/badge number, etc.) _____
7. Did Agent furnish a copy of the law or regulation requiring you to disclose the requested information? Yes/No
8. Is disclosure of the requested information voluntary or mandatory?
   _____
9. What use is to be made of the requested information?
   _____
10. What other agencies may have access to this information?
    _____
11. What is the result of choosing not to answer all or some of the questions? _____
12. Is the information requested of me part of an investigation?
    _____

13. Have you received information from any third party, record, or agency about me? Yes/No
If yes, identify all such persons, records, and agencies.

_____

_____

14. Do you reasonably anticipate any criminal or civil action to be initiated or pursued against me based on the information you seek? Yes/No

15. Is there any system of records, files, reports, or information about me maintained by your agency? Yes/No

16. Will you/your agency guarantee that information I provide will not be released to any other agency or person outside your agency without my express written authorization? Yes/No

Affirmation by Government Agent: I swear or affirm that the answers I have given to the forgoing questions are true and complete.

Signature: _____ Date: _____

Witness: _____ Date: _____

Chapter 9

PROTECTING YOUR PRIVACY IN THE MAIL

What you receive in the mail and with whom you communicate using the mail should be nobody's concern except your own. Furthermore, use of the mail should not reveal or lead to discovery of other aspects of your private life.

The United States Postal Service has recognized the importance of privacy and has adopted a policy designed to protect your privacy when using the U.S. mail. Title 39 Code of Federal Regulations Section 266 states in part the following:

Sec. 266.1 Purpose and scope.

This part is intended to protect individual privacy and affects all personal information collection and usage activities of the entire U.S. Postal Service. This includes the information interface of Postal Service employees to other employees, to individuals from the public at large, and to any private organization or governmental agency. [40 FR 45723, Oct. 2, 1975]

Sec. 266.2 Policy.

It is the policy of the U.S. Postal Service to ensure that any record within its custody that identifies or describes any characteristic or provides historical information about an individual or that affords a basis for inferring personal characteristics, or things done by or to such individual, including the record of any affiliation with an organization or activity, or admission to an institution, is accurate, complete, timely, relevant, and reasonably secure from unauthorized access. Additionally, it is the policy to provide the means for individuals to know: (a) Of the existence of all Postal Service Privacy Act systems of records, (b) the recipients and usage made of such information, (c) what information is optional or mandatory to provide to the Postal Service, (d) the procedures for individuals to review and request update to all information maintained about themselves, (e) the reproduction fees for releasing records, (f) the procedures for individual legal appeal in cases of dissatisfaction; and (g) of the establishment or revision of a computer matching program.

Unfortunately, what you receive in the mail can reveal a great deal about you. The magazines you subscribe to, the companies you do business with, the clubs and associations you belong to, and the organizations and individuals you communicate with can all lead to a development of a detailed profile of your life. It is not necessary to actually open and read your mail to start building this type of profile. By simply recording the information appearing on the outside of envelopes and packages (commonly called a "mail cover") received at your address an investigator can learn a great deal about your interests and associates.

Of course, the assumptions made by an investigator may not always be correct. The June 1998 issue of *Soldier of Fortune* magazine contains an article titled "Outrage" about Arthur Alphin and his wife, Elaine. Arthur, a retired U.S. Army lieutenant colonel, now a maker of custom big-game hunting rifles, and Elaine, an award-winning author of children's books, had their home raided by agents of the Bureau of Alcohol, Tobacco, and Firearms (BATF) on December 19, 1996. One of the stated reasons for the raid on the Alphin's home was they had received mail from a bank in Johannesburg, South Africa, and the BATF agents believed that the Alphins were engaged in money laundering. It turned out that the assumptions of the government agents were all wrong. The Alphins were charged with no crime and have no criminal record, yet their lives were irrevocably changed at the hands of government agents, based in part on a monitoring of their personal and business mail.

It isn't necessary for your mail to be monitored by a mail cover for you to end up in government records. If you had written a letter or two to Arthur Alphin to inquire about a custom hunting rifle during the time his mail was being monitored by the BATF, you were probably included in their reports as someone who had contact with the subject of their investigation. Could such contact lead to another investigation? Another raid?

To protect your privacy in the mail you should receive your mail at a post office box or mail drop service. To the greatest extent possible you should not associate your mail address with your residence address.

With the U.S. Postal Service you are required to show identification when renting a post office box and provide evidence of your residence address, which will be recorded on your box rental application.

When applying for a mailbox with a mail drop service, the Domestic Mail Manual, Regulation 153.211, requires that you fill out Postal Service Form 1583, Application for Delivery of Mail through Agent. Form 1583 requires that you provide your home address and telephone number. It also requires the mail drop operator to confirm your identity with two forms of identification and record those identifications on the form itself. Once you have completed the form, the mail drop operator keeps it on file and forwards a copy to the post office.

Some writers have suggested that you simply fill out Form 1583 with false or misleading information. It has been pointed out that some mail drop operators are not all that careful when it comes to confirming identification. Although you may be able to get away with providing false information to a mail drop operator, it is, in fact, illegal to deliberately provide false information on a federal form. Title 18, Section 1001, of the United States Code provides that if you are convicted of providing false information you may be fined up to $10,000 or imprisoned for up to five years or both. A warning to this effect is contained on Form 1583.

Even without providing any false information on Form 1583 there is an advantage to using a mail drop service to protect your privacy. One of the main advantages is that you can often structure your mailing address to appear to be a residence address when using a mail drop service. When using a mail drop service, mail for the area first arrives at the local post office. The post office then delivers (or the mail drop operator picks up from the post office) all mail going to the mail drop address. Say you have rented a mailbox from a mail drop operator located at 123 Main Street. You are assigned box 527. Your mailing address could read:

Mr. John Doe
123 Main Street, Apt. 527
Anytown, State 12345

Anyone not specifically familiar with 123 Main Street could reasonably believe this to be an apartment building, where you live in apartment 527. Most mail drops also receive deliveries for their customers from United Parcel Service or other shippers. They may also provide other such services as allowing you to call in to see whether you have received mail, telephone-answering service, and various mail-holding and forwarding services.

How safe is the information you provide on Form 1583 when renting a mail drop? Much depends on the mail drop operator. Any mail drop operator can be forced to turn over records because of a warrant or court order. The better mail drop operators will safeguard their records and not release any information unless presented with a warrant or court order; others will provide information to almost anyone with a plausible reason for asking. And, like anyone else, mail drop operators are just human and may be tricked, threatened, charmed, bribed, or conned into providing information about their customers.

The idea is to provide additional layers that someone must go through to get to you through your mailing address. If you establish your mail drop while living in an apartment in town, there is no reason to update your residence address when you move to a house in the suburbs. If no one at the apartment knows where you have moved, you have effectively created a dead end to tracing your residence through your mailing address.

Another option for receiving mail is to hire a secretarial service. Although dealing primarily with businesses and costing more than a mail drop service, a secretarial service does not require Form 1583 to receive mail. Secretarial services will also provide telephone-answering, typing, mailing, and other services generally required by businesses. Both mail drops (mailbox rental services) and secretarial services are listed in the business section of your telephone directory. Anyone seeking personal privacy would do well to look into the benefits of using one or both of these services.

It may be possible for you to arrange for a trusted friend to receive your mail. Assuming that your friend can be counted on not to divulge your whereabouts and is smart enough not to be tricked into doing so, you have a fairly safe way to receive your mail. The friend can bundle your mail and send it to you every few days or simply hold it for you until you can retrieve it. Be sure that in addition to trusting your friend you are sure that his family can also be counted on to be discreet about your whereabouts.

No matter where you receive your mail, it can be annoying to find your mailbox stuffed with advertisements and other junk mail every time you go to pick up your mail. This happens because many companies rent, share, or sell their mailing lists to other businesses. If you subscribe to a magazine, request information from a company about its product, or purchase something through the mail, it is highly likely that you will be added to someone's mailing list, and that list may be provided to other businesses.

For more information about how mailing lists are compiled, send a stamped, self-addressed envelope for the consumer booklet *Opening the Door to Opportunity* to the following:

Direct Marketing Association
Consumer Services—*Opening the Door*
1111 19th Street, NW
Suite 1100
Washington, DC 20036

Mail is only junk mail if you don't want to receive it. If you are interested in the products of a company, you may also be interested in the products of the companies with which it shares its mailing list. If this is not the case there are some things you should do.

When dealing with any particular company, request that it not provide your name and address to other companies as part of its mailing list. Many companies have a section on their order forms that allows you to check a box if you do not want your name and address released. If there is no such section on the form to make this request, simply include a note on the order form or other correspondence with the company.

If you do not want to receive advertising in the mail generally, contact the Direct Marketing Association (DMA) and ask that the organization add you to its "Do Not Mail" file. Several times a year the DMA sends this list to its subscribing companies, and the companies remove any addresses on this list from their advertising mailing list. This saves subscribers time and money by not mailing to individuals who don't want to receive their advertisements, and it means that you don't have to sort through piles of junk mail every time you pick up your mail.

To be removed from the mailing lists of those companies who subscribe to DMA, send your request to

Direct Marketing Association
Mail Preference Service
P.O. Box 9008
Farmingdale, NY 11735

On occasion you may receive sexually oriented advertising in the mail. If you do not wish to receive this type of advertising, you can apply to the U.S. Postal Service to be removed from the mailing lists of these companies. To stop

Chapter 10

▼

PROTECTING YOUR TELEPHONE PRIVACY

A telephone is not a secure means of communication. Every time you make a telephone call, the number, the date, the time, and the length of the call are recorded by the telephone company. This can be clearly seen by looking at your long-distance telephone bill at the end of the month. Another little-known fact is that the same information is recorded about your local calls. Known as message unit details by the telephone company, these records are maintained for at least six months.

During the course of an investigation, your telephone records would be available to law enforcement personnel. However, your telephone records may also be released to private investigators or others who have developed a contact in the telephone company. Although your telephone records should never be released without a warrant, you would be naive to believe that such has not happened or never could happen.

Another problem encountered with a telephone is that with a standard listed number, everyone knows who you are and where you live. Anyone who wants to can simply look up your telephone number and call you or drop by for a visit if your address is also listed in the directory. Of course, the first step in obtaining telephone privacy is to get an unlisted number. This will not defeat a determined investigator, but it will keep the general public from being able to locate you from a telephone directory.

Once you have an unlisted number, you must keep it private. You should give your home telephone number only to people you know and trust and whom you would be glad to hear from at anytime. When giving your private number to friends and family, be sure they understand that it is to be kept private.

There will be a number of occasions where you will be asked for a telephone number by people you would not want to have your private number. Think about places where your telephone number gets recorded and passed around: the employees' list at the office, the library, the local video store, the dry-cleaner's, the student roster at the community college where you took an evening class, or any number of other places.

If you provide your telephone number every time someone asks for it, you defeat the purpose of maintaining an unlisted number. There may be occasions when you want to provide a contact number to some person or business but don't wish to give out your private number. The solution is voice mail. By obtaining a voice mail number, you have a public number you can provide on those occasions when it may be necessary to provide a contact number, but when you don't want to provide your private telephone number. Another advantage of voice mail is that it allows you to screen your calls, and you can choose to respond to your voice mail messages or not.

The companies that provide voice mail services are found in the business section of the telephone directory, usually under "voice mail" or "paging services."

There is another way your private telephone number can be released without your permission: caller ID. Your telephone number can now be displayed to any party you call. For instance, order a pizza from your home and your telephone number gets displayed on the computer screen and becomes part of the business record of the local pizza delivery service. Place an order with a mail-order company, donate money to a charity, or request information about a product or service, and it is possible that your telephone number is automatically recorded through caller ID. Many of these companies sell or rent their customer lists, thereby providing your private telephone number to any number of other businesses.

To counter the problems associated with caller ID, you need number blocking, a service that prevents your telephone number from being displayed on a caller ID system. Number blocking comes in two forms: per call blocking and per line blocking. Per call blocking requires that you enter a code when making the call (*67 or something similar) to turn on number blocking. Per line blocking automatically performs number blocking on all calls made from a specific telephone line.

There probably is per line blocking installed on your private telephone line. No one should be able to record your private telephone number without your permission; however, there are occasions when number blocking does not work. If you dial 911 for emergency services, your telephone number will be automatically displayed to the emergency services dispatcher; if you call a toll-free number (800, 877, 888) or a service number (900) your telephone number is recorded as part of the telephone records of the firm using the prefixes.

Once your private number begins to circulate among various businesses and service providers, it is likely that it will be picked up by telemarketers, and you may start receiving calls from these companies, which will, of course, try to interest you in their products or services. (Telemarketing is not necessarily a bad thing, but you should not have to get calls from anyone unless you choose to.) In response to this, DMA has established a "telephone preference service." Most major telemarketers participate. By contacting DMA you can be added to its "do not call" list. Reputable telemarketers subscribing to the telephone preference service will not call any telephone number listed on the "do not call" list, which is updated four times a year: January, April, July, and October. Once added to the list, your name remains on file for five years.

To be added to DMA's do not call/delete list, contact it at

Direct Marketing Association
Telephone Preference Service
P.O. Box 9014
Farmingdale, NY 11735

When making telephone calls you don't want traced to you, call only from a pay phone and either use enough coins to make your call or use a prepaid calling card. Do not bill the call to a credit card or a third party.

Prepaid calling cards are available in many stores. You purchase a card with a certain number of minutes or units of calling time. With your prepaid calling card you dial a service number and receive a computer response. You then enter the number you wish to call and the account number on your prepaid calling card. At the end of your call the computer deducts the amount of time from the account on the card. When you have used all the allotted time on the card the account no longer works. As long as you're not found with the calling card in your possession, calls made from the prepaid account associated with the card can't be traced to you.

Cellular telephones add one more problem to maintaining your privacy. Whenever a cellular telephone is on it transmits a signal saying in effect, "Here I am." The cellular telephone transmits this signal to the nearest cell site. In rural areas cell sites may be several miles apart, but in cities the intervening distance is likely to be no more than several blocks. This information is recorded by telephone company computers, thereby allowing your location to be generally identified and your movements tracked. This information was already used by police in Switzerland to track the location of cellular telephone users. Beginning in the year 2001, the Federal Communications Commission (FCC) has mandated that as part of its Enhanced 911 (E-911) program a cellular telephone company must be able to pinpoint a 911 caller's location to within 125 meters anywhere in the United States. Once the E-911 system is fully on line, it will be no problem to track a particular cellular telephone simply by its cell site locating signal.

Chapter 11

PROTECTING THE PRIVACY
OF YOUR HOME

There is an old saying that a man's home is his castle. The privacy of one's own home should be sacred. What one does in the privacy of his own home is no one's business but his own! Although the Fourth Amendment to the Constitution uses the word "houses" and not "home," the meaning is clear:

> The right of the people to be secure in their persons, houses, papers, and effects, against unreasonable searches and seizures, shall not be violated, and no Warrants shall issue, but upon probable cause, supported by Oath or affirmation, and particularly describing the place to be searched, and the persons or things to be seized.

The instruction here is clearly directed toward the government. No private citizen has any right to invade the sanctity of your home, and, according to the Constitution of the United States, government agents may do so only with a warrant, based upon probable cause, which is supported by oath or affirmation. If you are ever in a situation where an agent of the government wants to search your person, home, papers, or effects, you are entitled to be presented with a warrant showing the authority to do so. However, one must remember that the Fourth Amendment protects against *unreasonable* searches and seizures. The courts have held that there are various types of searches and seizures that are, in fact, *reasonable* and therefore not protected under the Fourth Amendment. The application of the Fourth Amendment under law is a study in and of itself, and volumes could be filled (and have been filled) on just this one topic.

An important definition concerning privacy in one's home is *curtilage*. According to *Black's Law Dictionary*, 6th edition, curtilage is

> . . . a word derived from the Latin cohors (a place enclosed around a yard) and the old French cortilliage or courtillage, which today has been corrupted into court-yard. Originally, it referred to the land and outbuildings immediately adjacent to a castle that were in turn surrounded by a high stone wall; today, its meaning has been extended to include any land or building immediately adjacent to a dwelling, and usually it is enclosed some way by a fence or shrubs. (*U.S. v. Romano*, D.C. Pa., 388 F. Supp. 101, 104)
>
> For search and seizure purposes, it includes those outbuildings that are directly and intimately connected with the habitation (and in proximity thereto) and the land or grounds surrounding

the dwelling which are necessary and convenient
and habitually used for family purposes and carrying on domestic employment. (*State v. Hanson*,
113 N.H. 689, 313 A.2d 730, 732)

This means that the privacy of your home is extended to
those buildings and areas over which you maintain clear
control and which you habitually use as part of your daily
life. Thus your garage, next to your house, is likely protected under the definition of curtilage, but a storage shed on
the far side of your 10-acre lot probably is not. Although no
one should be allowed to trespass into your storage shed,
you do not have the same Fourth Amendment protections
in the storage shed that you do in those areas in the curtilage of your home.

Your home is the one place where you should have total
control over your environment. This provides a great
advantage in securing your personal privacy while at home.

One of the first steps for providing at-home privacy is to
make your home physically secure. This means that you
should have strong doors with good dead-bolt locks, secure
windows, proper lighting, etc. These things are most commonly thought of as crime prevention techniques, and of
course they are, but they also keep uninvited "guests" from
having a look around your place to see what they can dis-
cover. Remember, it is not unheard of for unscrupulous private investigators, bad cops, or nosy neighbors and land-
lords to enter someone's home on a bit of a fishing expedi-
tion. Clearly this is illegal, but once it has happened it may
be impossible to recover your lost privacy. Therefore, you
should make it as difficult as possible for anyone to enter
your home uninvited.

Now take a look at your home from the outside. What
can be seen from the public street? From adjoining property? From the air? There can be no real expectation of pri-

vacy if you, in effect, put something on display to the public. Do you have a couple of "assault rifles" hanging on the wall of your den? Are you engaged in a little amateur agriculture in the backyard, maybe growing a couple of marijuana plants? Do you meet regularly with friends in your home to discuss something that may not be "politically correct"? If you answered yes to any of these or other similar questions, you should consider whether your activities can be observed from outside your home. What if the person doing the eavesdropping is using binoculars or a parabolic microphone?

There is no need to become overly paranoid or live in a deep, dark cave to protect the privacy of your home, but it is important to be aware of what may be observed by those who care to look in from the outside.

Along this same line, take care what you discard. Once you throw something into the trash and set it on the curb to be hauled away, you have abandoned it. There is nothing to prevent someone from collecting your trash and going through it to see what he can learn. In fact, trash analysis is a common investigative technique used by police and intelligence agencies. Think about what you throw in the trash and what could be learned from it. Have you thrown out credit card statements, bank statements, old prescription bottles? Your receipt from the grocery store probably itemizes every item you purchased. Empty liquor or wine bottles may profile what you drink and how often. Before you discard items into your trash, be sure to shred or burn any papers that may provide information about you. Sort your trash into separate containers and take bottles, cans, and such to recycling centers. This will enhance your privacy, and it's good for the environment. Anyone who goes through your trash looking for information should come up with nothing more than a handful of old coffee grounds, the scraps from last night's dinner, and the baby's dirty Pampers.

Finally, be careful whom you invite into your home. Of course, your family and close friends should be welcome, but you should be wary of strangers seeking entry. Make it a personal policy never to conduct business in your home. You probably don't need or really even want anything being peddled by a door-to-door salesman. Your insurance and investment needs will likely be better served by companies that actually have a business office. If you want to get religion, go to church. If you are feeling charitable, mail a donation to your favorite charity, but don't invite someone going door to door to come in and have a seat while you look for a little spare cash.

The bottom line is that your home should be a place of safety, security, and privacy. Take special care to protect it.

pany e-mail account, but these things are still the property of your employer. Your access to the property of your employer is for the purposes of doing your job. If you maintain personal information in a file on your company's computer or store personal items in your desk drawer at the office, you have little expectation of privacy in these places. Your employer is usually justified in examining these places in the course of normal business activities. For example, if you keep a personal diary in your desk at work, and while you are away on vacation a co-worker looks in your desk drawer for a company file and finds your diary, you have no recourse in this matter. You have no expectation of privacy in your desk drawer.

If, however, you have a personal briefcase that you bring to the office with you that is not used primarily for company business, even if you leave the briefcase at your office when you go on vacation, you do have a reasonable expectation of privacy concerning the items inside it. Your co-worker or supervisor has no right to search your briefcase.

However, let's now consider a locker assigned to you by your employer. The locker is used by you to store personal items while at work. There is no reason for you to store company property in the locker. Does your employer have a right to open your locker and examine its contents? This question was examined by the courts in *K-Mart Corporation Store No. 7441 v. Trotti* 677 S.W.2d 632 (1984). In this case an employee of K-Mart had been assigned a locker in which she stored her personal items while engaged in the conduct of her employment as a salesclerk in the store. The store manager and security personnel conducted a search of the store lockers in an attempt to locate a missing watch and various items of company property. Trotti was not suspected in the theft of the property, but her locker was searched along with other lockers at the store. The jury awarded her $8,000 in actual damages and $100,000 in exemplary damages for invasion of her privacy. Trotti had in this case demonstrated a reasonable expectation of privacy by placing a lock on her locker and maintaining control over it, with consent of the store. Although this case was, on appeal, remanded for a new trial, based largely on the amount of exemplary damages awarded, it is clear that juries consider privacy important in those cases where a reasonable expectation of privacy can be demonstrated.

If you work in a large business and have an office e-mail account, it is likely that your e-mail is being read by someone in management. In his May 23, 1993, column in the *Chicago Tribune/Tribune Business News*, James Coates reported, "More than 30 percent of companies with 1,000 employees or more responded that they routinely conduct searches—the equivalent of the boss unlocking your desk, taking out your diary, and perusing anything that looked interesting. Worse, 60 percent of a large sampling of people in charge of computer operations in America . . . don't see anything wrong with that."

It is frightening to think that one-third of the people working in major business routinely have their private communications monitored by their employers, but it is even more frightening that a majority of people in charge of the computer systems used in this monitoring don't see anything wrong with it. We've reached the point where it has become a matter of policy and is commonly accepted to pry into the privacy of others.

Chapter 13

PROTECTING YOUR PRIVACY IN THE MILITARY

Military service is a unique and honorable profession. Those who choose to serve their country as members of the military swear to support and defend the Constitution of the United States against all enemies, both foreign and domestic. Defending the nation against foreign enemies is easily understood. Fighting the nation's wars, protecting the nation from invasion, is the bottom-line job of the armed forces. But what about domestic enemies, who are they and can we be expect to be defended against them? Certainly spies, traitors, and terrorists are domestic enemies, but there may be a more subtle domestic enemy of which our service members must be aware and act to defend against. This subtle enemy is those in the military and its supporting agencies who ignore the rights and freedoms guaranteed to all people by the Constitution of the United States in the name of policy and procedure. Soldiers, sailors, airmen, and marines do not surrender their Constitutional rights and freedoms by virtue of their oath to defend these rights and freedoms from attack by the nation's enemies.

As a member of the armed forces you enjoy the same Constitutional rights and freedoms as those citizens you protect. We have already seen that the right of privacy is a personal and fundamental right protected by the Constitution, and that where rights secured by the Constitution are involved there can be no rulemaking or legislation that abrogates them. Unfortunately, many in the military bureaucracy choose to ignore those rights and freedoms with regard to service members.

Policy and procedure cannot circumvent our nation's laws. There is generally no exemption for the military when it comes to complying with privacy laws: the Privacy Act of 1974 applies to the military services just as it does to all other federal agencies.

The Privacy Act was passed for the purpose of curtailing the expanding use of SSNs . . . and to eliminate the threat to individual privacy and confidentiality posed by common numerical identifiers. Yet military personnel are required to disclose their SSNs for almost every activity they wish to take part in while serving in the armed forces. To make matters worse, the military services make little or no effort to protect this information once it is obtained from the service member, even though by law and their own regulations they are required to do so.

The law states that "no agency shall disclose any record which is contained in a system of records by any means of communication to any person, or to another agency, except pursuant to a written request by, or with the prior written consent of, the individual to whom the record pertains . . ." This applies to military agencies, not just all other agencies of the federal government. The problem faced by military personnel is that information about them is freely exchanged between various agencies and disclosed to unit commanders without the consent of the service member even being sought, much less having been obtained by prior written consent.

Military members should become familiar with the Privacy Act of 1974. Furthermore, each service member should review his service's regulations covering obtaining, maintaining, and disclosing personal information. Where regulations, policies, and procedures conflict with existing U.S. laws and the Constitutionally protected right to privacy, every service member has a duty and a responsibility to challenge this illegal disregard for his rights and freedoms.

Concerning the rights of public employees, the Supreme Court stated in the Garriety case (*Garriety v. New Jersey*, 87 S. Ct. 616, 620 [1967]) that they "are not relegated to a watered-down version of Constitutional rights." Public employees, and this includes the men and women defending this great nation in the armed forces, are not deprived of their Constitutional rights by virtue of their duties or employment. Any policy or regulation that deprives a service member of his Constitutional rights and freedoms is unlawful.

The various military services often claim that their actions are governed by specific regulations and policies necessary to the functioning of the armed forces. Generally this is true, and military rules, order, and discipline should not be compared directly with the civilian counterparts. However, when it comes to those rights and freedoms protected by the Constitution, there can be no watering down of those rights simply because one is in military service. As we have already seen, privacy is a right protected by the Constitution and no rule or regulation may be lawfully made which abrogates those rights.

The right of privacy is a personal and fundamental right protected by the Constitution of the

United States. Section 2 of Public Law 93-579, paragraph (a)(4).

Where rights secured by the Constitution are involved, there can be no rule making or legislation which would abrogate them. (*Miranda v. Arizona*, 384 U.S. 436, 491)

In researching this section the author filed an FOIA request to determine what law or regulation authorized a U.S. Air Force agency to collect individuals' SSNs as part of its function to provide morale and welfare services to its supported air force community. In response to the FOIA request the author received a reply from the Department of the Air Force, 86th Airlift Wing (USAFE), that stated in part: "An extensive search was conducted to locate the materials you requested. Specifically, the law which authorizes the (Name of Agency) to collect social security numbers . . . The result of that search was 'no records found.'"

This would indicate that you do not have to give your SSN to identify yourself. Clearly the solicitation of SSNs by this air force agency was merely a matter of policy and not authorized by law. This violated the intent of the Privacy Act, as well as putting military members at risk from the extensive disclosure of their SSNs for unauthorized purposes. Hopefully, the 86th Airlift Wing will take steps to limit this threat to air force members; however, at the time this book was submitted for publication the air force had not changed its policy.

The military services do, in fact, have a privacy program, based on Department of Defense Directive 5400.11, DoD Privacy Program. Let's take a look at Army Regulation 340-21, "The Army Privacy Program," as an example of one of the military service's privacy protection regulations.

Army Regulation 340-21 states: "This regulation applies to the Active Army, the Army National Guard, the U.S. Army Reserve, and the Army and Air Force Exchange Service."

Basically, this means that it applies to everyone in the army, from the commanding general to the post exchange clerk. The regulation further states that it is army policy to protect the privacy of individuals from unwarranted intrusion; to collect only the personal information about an individual that is legally authorized and necessary to support army operations; to safeguard personal information to prevent unauthorized use, access, disclosure, alteration, or destruction; and to let individuals know what records the army keeps on them and allow them to review or get copies of these records. As with most privacy laws and regulations, the army seems to have a reasonable policy: collect only what is necessary for operations, safeguard it from unauthorized disclosure, and let the individuals concerned review their records for completeness and accuracy. Unfortunately, the intent of this regulation is too often ignored by those who have not bothered to find out, or simply don't care, about the privacy rights of our servicemen and women.

The regulation goes on to state that "the Army is prohibited from disclosing a record from a system of records without obtaining the prior written consent of the data subject . . ." The term *data subject* is defined as "the individual about who[m] the army is maintaining information in a system of records." There are various exemptions to the release of information without obtaining prior written consent, such as release to the Bureau of the Census, or when the information is used solely as statistical research or transferred in a form that is not individually identifiable. Generally, however, the army has no right to release information about you to a third party.

The military services are required to provide a service

member with a Privacy Act Statement that details their authority to collect the request information, the principal purposes for which the information will be used, and the probable routine uses of the information collected "whenever personal information is requested from an individual that will become part of a system of records retrieved by reference to the individual's name or other personal identifier." Concerning the Privacy Act Statement, the regulation states that "in certain instances, it may be printed in a public notice in a conspicuous location such as at check-cashing facilities; however, if the individual requests a copy of the contents, it must be provided." The author recommends that service members request and receive a written copy of the Privacy Act Statement whenever their personal information is requested.

We have already mentioned how the SSN is used as a universal identifier for military members, but is such use actually authorized? Concerning the SSN, army regulation 340-21 states:

> Executive Order 9397 authorizes DA [Department of the Army] to use the SSN as a system to identify Army members and employees. Once a military member or civilian employee of DA has disclosed his or her SSN for the purposes of establishing personnel, financial, or medical records upon entry into the Army service or employment, the SSN becomes his or her identification number. No other use of this number is authorized. Therefore, whether the SSN alone is requested from the individual, or the SSN together with other personal information, the Privacy Act Statement must make clear that disclosure of the number is voluntary. If the individual refuses to disclose the SSN, the Army activity must be prepared to identify the individual by alternate means.

What the regulation seems to be saying here is that with the exception of your personnel (201 file), finance, and medical records, you are not required to disclose your SSN. Military regulations and U.S. laws provide reasonable protection for the privacy of our service members only when those laws are applied and enforced. Looking one last time at Army Regulation 340-21 we see the following:

The Privacy Act has both civil and criminal penalties for violations of its provisions.

    a. Civil remedies. An individual may file a civil suit against the Army if army personnel fail to comply with the Privacy Act.

    b. Criminal penalties. A member or employee of the Army may be found guilty of a misdemeanor and fined not more than $5,000.00 for willfully—

        (1) Maintaining a system of records without first meeting public notice requirements of publishing in the Federal Register.

        (2) Disclosing individually identifiable personal information to one not entitled to it.

        (3) Asking for or getting another's record under false pretenses.

Violations of the rights and freedoms of our service members should be addressed through the military chain of command. Each military service has an inspector general who is charged with ensuring that his service acts within the law and that the rights and freedoms of the service members are protected. Finally, every service member has elected representatives in government to whom he may

Chapter 14

PROTECTING YOUR PRIVACY WHEN CONFRONTED BY THE POLICE

What should you do when confronted by the police? The answer to this question depends on the type of involvement you have with the police. Basically, there are three types of contact with the police that you do not initiate yourself.

CASUAL CONTACT

The first type of contact is *casual*, where a police officer approaches you in a public place and initiates some kind of contact with you. This can be as simple as beginning a conversation with you as you sit in a coffee shop or shop in a mall. During a casual contact there is no requirement for you to answer the police officer's questions, engage him in any type of conversation, or remain in his presence. You are clearly free to ignore him and leave the area. The question to immediately ask yourself when contacted by the police is, "Why did the cop want to talk to me?" Police officers are human, and just like anyone else may start up a conversation with someone they meet on the street. On the other hand, police are never really off duty. When the conversation proceeds beyond "good morning, nice weather," it's time to consider carefully the questions you are being asked and why. By talking with the police you create the possibility of giving the police officer a reasonable suspicion to detain you.

DETENTION

The second type of contact with the police is *detention*. In detention you have not been arrested, but you are not free to leave either. For a police officer to detain you he must have a reasonable suspicion that you are involved in some way in some type of criminal activity. This does not mean that the police officer has probable cause to arrest you, but he does have a suspicion that, under the circumstances, it is reasonable to believe criminal activity is at hand. In this case it is likely that you have done something to attract the attention of the police, such as fleeing at the sight of the police, attempting to conceal something from their view, or wearing a disguise. It can also include being in a "high crime" area, associating with known criminals, or being out of place in a neighborhood. For example, if you are poorly dressed and walking down the street in a wealthy neighborhood at 3 A.M., a police officer may have reasonable suspicion to detain you even though there is nothing illegal about being poorly dressed and walking down a public street at 3 A.M. The courts have held that a detention is an intermediate level of intrusion. You are not free to leave, but you are generally not required to produce identification or answer questions.

A detention must be reasonably brief in nature, no more than 20 to 30 minutes. An hour is clearly too long, and the further past the 30-minute limit the detention is, the less reasonable it becomes to detain you. Furthermore, in a detention you may not be forcibly moved to another location (forcible movement of you to any location constitutes arrest). In a detention the police officer is looking for probable cause to arrest you. If he can determine no probable cause, he must let you go.

ARREST

The third and most serious type of contact with the police is *arrest*. To arrest you a police officer must have probable cause. The courts have stated the following:

> Probable cause to arrest exists where facts and circumstances within officers' knowledge and of which they had reasonably trustworthy information are sufficient in themselves to warrant a person of reasonable caution in the belief that an offense has been or is being committed; it is not necessary that the officer possesses knowledge of facts to establish guilt, but more than mere suspicion is required. (*State v. Phillips*, 67 Hawaii 535, 696 P.2d 346, 350)

This means that there must clearly be more evidence pointing to the fact that you have committed an offense than there is against it. Once you have been arrested you will be taken to the police station where you will be "booked." Following your arrest you will be informed of your rights. Although there may be slight variances in the exact wording of your rights advisement, basically you will be told the following:

1. You do not have to answer questions or say anything.

2. Anything you say or do can be used as evidence against you in a criminal trial.

3. You have a right to talk with a lawyer before or after questioning or have a lawyer present with you during questioning. If you cannot afford a lawyer and want one, arrangements will be made to obtain a lawyer for you.

4. If you are willing to discuss the offense(s) under investigation, with or without a lawyer present, you have a right to stop answering questions at any time or speak to a lawyer before answering further, even if you sign a waiver certificate.

If you are ever read your rights, **ask for a lawyer and then shut up**. There is absolutely nothing to be gained by talking with the police or investigators. Once the police have probable cause to arrest you, they believe you are guilty of a crime. Anything you say can be used against you, so say nothing. Being arrested is one of the most serious invasions of privacy you can face. Under the circumstances you will not be thinking clearly. Under the stress of arrest you will be likely to tear down the walls of privacy you have built for yourself. Again, if things have degenerated to the point of your being arrested, make no statements except in the presence of your attorney and do your best to salvage whatever is left of your privacy.

SEARCH AND SEIZURE

We read what the Fourth Amendment to the Constitution had to say about search and seizure in Chapter 11. Basically, for the police to search a place where you have a reasonable expectation of privacy they must have a warrant. However, there are exceptions to this rule. The main exception we are concerned with here is consent. If you consent to officers' searching your property, they need no warrant. During casual contact or a detention police may ask permission to search (e.g., "Would you mind if I look through the trunk of your car?" "What's in your briefcase? Would you mind opening it up so I can look?"). With regard to these requests—**never consent to a search**. The police may tell you that they can get a warrant. If that is the case, require them do so.

The ACLU provides several tips about what you should do if you're stopped by the police:

- Be polite. Never become verbally abusive with the police officer. Becoming verbally abusive can result in your being arrested.

- Keep your hands where they can be seen.

- Don't run or attempt to hide from the police.

- Don't complain or tell the police officer that he is wrong or that you are going to file a complaint.

- Do **not** make any statement about the incident. If you are arrested, ask for a lawyer immediately.

- Memorize the police officers' names, badge numbers, patrol car number, etc. You must be able to positively identify the police officers you dealt with.

- If you feel that your rights have been violated by the police, file a written complaint with the police department's internal affairs division, civilian review board, and other local agencies dealing with police conduct and procedures.

- If you are stopped for questioning, you don't have to answer the police officer's questions. However, not answering any questions may make the police suspicious of you.

- If stopped on the street, you generally can't be arrested for refusing to identify yourself (check your local ordinances regarding requirements to identify yourself to the police). If you are driving an automobile, you must show your driver's license and vehicle registration, but there is no requirement to answer further questions.

- If the police believe you are carrying a concealed weapon, they may "pat you down" (called a "Terry Frisk"). **Never consent to a search of your person, automobile, home, or anyplace else where you may have a reasonable expectation of privacy**. If the police claim that they have a warrant, ask to see it and read it.

- If you are arrested, the police will search you and the immediate area around you. The immediate area around you means places you can quickly reach, e.g., the room or vehicle in which you are arrested.

Chapter 15

THE REALITY OF PRIVACY ACTIVISM

Throughout this book we have looked at several aspects of privacy and the various laws and regulations that are designed to protect our privacy. Having read this far, you are aware of your clear right to privacy; however, the majority of bureaucrats are unaware of your privacy rights or simply don't care about them.

When you attempt to assert your privacy rights you will stand out from the crowd. The majority of people in today's society are herded along like so many sheep, blatting out their personal and private information every time someone asks for it or slides a form under their noses. When you protest this clear invasion of your rights and freedoms you will stand out from the herd—you will no longer be one of the mindless sheep.

The idea is to assert your privacy rights without drawing an undue amount of attention to yourself. Many of the suggestions for protecting your privacy make use of common services (such as voice mail or postal money orders) and don't attract any particular attention. Other things I have suggested (such as not disclosing your SSN) may attract attention. Why didn't you just answer all their questions and blurt out your private and personal details because they demanded such of you? You're not one of the mindless sheep!

To protect your privacy rights and freedoms, begin by employing all the techniques that attract no particular attention. When enforcing your privacy rights under the law, deal quietly and professionally with those who are in a position to understand the law and act in accordance with its requirements. You will accomplish little by arguing with bureaucrats about the necessity of filling out the pile of forms they push in front of you. You don't have to comply with their mindless demands, but they are not the ones to change the policy.

To effect changes in policy it is necessary to address your concerns to supervisors and management. Meet with these people and clearly and politely explain your concerns about the loss of privacy rights and freedoms. Send letters to general managers and corporate heads citing the laws that protect privacy rights and explain how their current policy violates these laws and endangers the rights, freedoms, and safety of their customers.

Quality businesses will make considerable effort to protect the rights of their customers once they are aware that their customers consider these issues important. Those few businesses that disregard your concerns probably don't deserve your business anyway. Boycott them and urge that your friends do the same. Businesses that ignore the concerns of their customers don't stay in business very long.

When dealing with government agencies, you may find that they are less concerned with the wishes of the people than a business that depends on the community for its existence, but pressure may still be put on those agencies that disregard the rights and freedoms of "We the People." Whenever you must deal with an uncaring bureaucrat, get that person's name and job title and file appropriate letters of complaint. Remember, government officials receive performance evaluations, which are considered when promotions and pay raises are proposed. Well-written letters, clearly documenting the employees' disregard for the law, do not sit well in their personnel files. Use the FOIA to require agencies to show clear authority for their actions that influence your privacy rights and freedoms. If an agency cannot document a clear and specific exemption to privacy laws, insist that it immediately cease and desist in those actions that harm your privacy rights. Remember, government agencies have no right to violate the law (even if they sometimes get away with doing so).

Chapter 16

15 STEPS TO PRIVACY

1. Develop a privacy-focused attitude. Make privacy a part of your life and your dealings with others.

2. Receive mail at a post office box or through a mail drop. Do not have mail delivered to your home.

3. Have an unlisted telephone number at your home. Give your home telephone number only to close friends and family.

4. Use a voice mail number as your business/public telephone number.

5. Install per line call blocking on your home telephone. Don't call toll-free numbers from your home telephone.

6. Use prepaid calling cards and place calls from a public telephone (pay phone) for your sensitive calls.

7. Use postal money orders for purchases or payments when you obviously cannot send cash. Do not use checks.

8. If you must use a checking account, the only personal information that should be printed on your check is your name. For instance, do not have your address, telephone number, SSN, or driver's license number printed on your personal checks.

9. Never disclose your SSN unless specifically required to do so by law. Do not allow it to be used as an account number.

10. Contact the Direct Marketing Association and request that your name be removed from mailing lists and telephone marketing call lists.

11. Request a copy of your credit report from each of the major credit reporting agencies at least once per year. Carefully review your credit reports for completeness and accuracy and correct any errors.

12. Get Pretty Good Privacy encryption software and use it in your electronic communications (e-mail). Send e-mail through anonymous remailers. Establish one or more Web-based e-mail accounts.

13. Be aware of what you throw in the trash. Shred or burn any invoices, bank statements, personal letters, credit card statements, preapproved applications, and all other similar information.

14. Avoid predictability in your personal routine. Use different routes to travel between home and work each day. Vary stores you shop, the restaurants where you eat, and the service stations where you buy gasoline.

15. Be a privacy advocate. Work to change laws, rules, regulations, policies, and procedures that adversely affect personal privacy. Contact your elected representatives about privacy issues. Protest violations of your privacy rights and freedoms. Join and support privacy advocacy groups and organizations.

APPENDIX A

TABLE OF CASES, LAWS, AND REGULATIONS CITED

- Public Law 93-579 (5 U.S.C. 552a), the Privacy Act of 1974

- *Miranda v. Arizona*, 384 U.S. 436, 491

- *Harvard Law Review*, "The Right to Privacy" 1890 Harv.L.Rev. 193

- *CNA Financial Corporation v. Local 743*, D.C., Ill., 1981, 515F, Supp. 942, Ill.

- *Doyle v. Wilson*, D.C., Del., 1982, 529G, Supp. 1343

- *Greidinger v. Davis*, 988 F.2d 1344 (4th Cir. 1993) 1345-53

- *Yager v. Hackensack Water Co.*, 615 F. Supp. 1087 (D.C., N.J. 1985)

- Executive Order 9397

- 10 U.S.C. Section 3012, 3013

- 10 U.S.C. Section 8012, 8013

- *Plyler v. Doe 457,* U.S. 202 (1982)

- 20 U.S.C. Section 1232g

- Section 1747.8 California Civil Code

- 5 U.S.C. Section 552

- Title 39 Code of Federal Regulations, Section 266

- Fourth Amendment to the U.S. Constitution

- *U.S. v. Romano,* D.C., Pa., 388 F. Supp. 101, 104

- *State v. Hanson,* 113 N.H. 689, 313 A. 2d 730, 732

- *K-Mart Corporation Store No. 7441 v. Trotti,* 677 S.W. 2d 632 (1984)

- *Garriety v. New Jersey,* 87 S. Ct. 616, 620 (1967)

- Department of Defense Directive 5400.11

- U.S. Army Regulation 340-21, the Army Privacy Program

- *State v. Phillips,* 67 Hawaii 535, 696 P. 2d 346, 350

APPENDIX B

PRIVACY INFORMATION RESOURCES

American Civil Liberties Union (ACLU)
132 West 43rd Street
New York, NY 10036
Web page: http://www.aclu.org

American Civil Liberties Union (ACLU)
122 Maryland Avenue, NE
Washington, DC 20002
E-mail: privaclu@aol.com

Center for Democracy & Technology
1634 I. Street, NW, #1,100
Washington, DC 20006
E-mail: info@cdt.org
Web page: http://www.cdt.org

Computer Professionals for Social Responsibility
P.O. Box 717
Palo Alto, CA 94302
E-mail: cpsr@cpsr.org
Web page: http://www.cpsr@cpsr.org

Electronic Frontier Foundation
1550 Bryant Street, #725
San Francisco, CA 94103
E-mail: ask@eff.org
Web page: http://www.eff.org

F.E.A.R. Foundation
(Forfeiture Endangers American Rights)
P.O. Box 15421
Washington, DC 20003
Web page: http://www.fear.org/

Federal Trade Commission
Consumer Response Center
Washington, DC 20580

Privacy International
666 Pennsylvania Avenue, SE, Number 301
Washington, DC 20003
E-mail: pi@privacy.org
Web page: http://www.privacy.org/pi

Privacy Rights Clearinghouse
5384 Linda Vista Road, Number 306
San Diego, CA 92110
E-mail: prc@privacyrights.org
Web page: http://www.privacyrights.org

Private Citizen, Inc.
P.O. Box 233
Naperville, IL 60566
E-mail: prvtctzn@private-citizen.com
Web page: http://www.private-citizen.com

U.S. Privacy Council
P.O. Box 15060
Washington, DC 20003

APPENDIX C

▼

FEDERAL LEGISLATION RELATING TO PRIVACY

- Freedom of Information Act (1966)—Ensures that individuals have the right to access information maintained about them in government files.

- Fair Credit Reporting Act (1970)—Ensures that consumers have the right to be informed about the nature and scope of credit investigations conducted about them and receive the names of firms that will be receiving this information.

- Crime Control Act (1973)—Safeguards the confidentiality of information maintained in state criminal investigation files.

- Family Educational Rights and Privacy Act (1974)—Limits access to information maintained about students by colleges and universities.

- Privacy Act (1974)—Protects the privacy rights of individuals about whom the federal government maintains information.

- Tax Reform Act (1976)—Safeguards the privacy of personal financial information.

- Right to Financial Privacy Act (1978)—Prohibits financial institutions from providing information about individuals to the federal government without the consent of the individual involved.

- Electronic Fund Transfer Act (1980)—Requires financial institutions to inform an individual if a third party gains access to the individual's account.

- Cable Communications Policy Act (1984)—Controls access to information collected by cable services about its customers.

- Electronic Communications Privacy Act (1986)—Prohibits interception of electronic communication.

- Video Privacy Protection Act (1988)—Prohibits disclosure of information maintained by video rental services about their customers.

APPENDIX D

THE PRIVACY ACT OF 1974 AND AMENDMENTS (AS OF JANUARY 2, 1991)

5 USC Sec. 552a
TITLE 5
PART I
CHAPTER 5
SUBCHAPTER II

Sec. 552a. Records maintained on individuals

  (a) Definitions. - For purposes of this section -

   (1) the term 'agency' means agency as defined in section 552(e) (FOOTNOTE 1) of this title; (FOOTNOTE 1) See References in Text note below.

   (2) the term 'individual' means a citizen of the United States or an alien lawfully admitted for permanent residence;

(3)   the term 'maintain' includes maintain, collect, use, or disseminate;

(4)   the term 'record' means any item, collection, or grouping of information about an individual that is maintained by an agency, including, but not limited to, his education, financial transactions, medical history, and criminal or employment history and that contains his name, or the identifying number, symbol, or other identifying particular assigned to the individual, such as a finger or voice print or a photograph;

(5)   the term 'system of records' means a group of any records under the control of any agency from which information is retrieved by the name of the individual or by some identifying number, symbol, or other identifying particular assigned to the individual;

(6)   the term 'statistical record' means a record in a system of records maintained for statistical research or reporting purposes only and not used in whole or in part in making any determination about an identifiable individual, except as provided by section 8 of title 13;

(7)   the term 'routine use' means, with respect to the disclosure of a record, the use of such record for a purpose which is compatible with the purpose for which it was collected;

(8)   the term 'matching program' -
   (A)   means any computerized comparison of -
      (i)   two or more automated systems of records or a system of records with non-Federal records for the purpose of -
         (I)   establishing or verifying the eligibility of, or continuing

                           compliance with statutory and regulatory requirements by, applicants for, recipients or beneficiaries of, participants in, or providers of services with respect to, cash or in-kind assistance or payments under Federal benefit programs, or

          (II)   recouping payments or delinquent debts under such

Federal benefit programs, or

          (ii)   two or more automated Federal personnel or payroll systems of records or a system of Federal personnel or payroll records with non-Federal records,

     (B)   but does not include -

          (i)   matches performed to produce aggregate statistical data without any personal identifiers;

          (ii)   matches performed to support any research or statistical project, the specific data of which may not be used to make decisions concerning the rights, benefits, or privileges of specific individuals;

          (iii) matches performed, by an agency (or component thereof) which performs as its principal function any activity pertaining to the enforcement of criminal laws, subsequent to the initiation of a specific criminal or civil law enforcement investigation of a named person or persons for the purpose of gathering evidence against such person or persons;

(iv) matches of tax information

    (I) pursuant to section 6103(d) of the Internal Revenue Code of 1986,

    (II) for purposes of tax administration as defined in section 6103(b)(4) of such Code,

    (III) for the purpose of intercepting a tax refund due an individual under authority granted by section 464 or 1137 of the Social Security Act; or

    (IV) for the purpose of intercepting a tax refund due an individual under any other tax refund intercept program authorized by statute which has been determined by the Director of the Office of Management and Budget to contain verification, notice, and hearing requirements that are substantially similar to the procedures in section 1137 of the Social Security Act;

(v) matches -

    (I) using records predominantly relating to Federal personnel, that are performed for routine administrative purposes (subject to guidance provided by the Director of the Office of Management and Budget pursuant to subsection (v)); or

    (II) conducted by an agency using only records from systems of

records maintained by that
agency; if the purpose of the
match is not to take any
adverse financial, personnel,
disciplinary, or other adverse
action against Federal personnel; or

(vi) matches performed for foreign
counterintelligence purposes or to
produce background checks for
security clearances of Federal personnel or Federal contractor personnel;

(9)   the term 'recipient agency' means any
agency, or contractor thereof, receiving
records contained in a system of records
from a source agency for use in a matching
program;

(10) the term 'non-Federal agency' means any
State or local government, or agency thereof,
which receives records contained in a system of records from a source agency for use
in a matching program;

(11) the term 'source agency' means any agency
which discloses records contained in a system of records to be used in a matching program, or any State or local government, or
agency thereof, which discloses records to
be used in a matching program;

(12) the term 'Federal benefit program' means
any program administered or funded by the
Federal Government, or by any agent or
State on behalf of the Federal Government,
providing cash or in-kind assistance in the
form of payments, grants, loans, or loan
guarantees to individuals; and

(13) the term 'Federal personnel' means officers

and employees of the Government of the United States, members of the uniformed services (including members of the Reserve Components), individuals entitled to receive immediate or deferred retirement benefits under any retirement program of the Government of the United States (including survivor benefits).

(b) Conditions of Disclosure. - No agency shall disclose any record which is contained in a system of records by any means of communication to any person, or to another agency, except pursuant to a written request by, or with the prior written consent of, the individual to whom the record pertains, unless disclosure of the record would be -

(1) to those officers and employees of the agency which maintains the record who have a need for the record in the performance of their duties;

(2) required under section 552 of this title;

(3) for a routine use as defined in subsection (a)(7) of this section and described under subsection (e)(4)(D) of this section;

(4) to the Bureau of the Census for purposes of planning or carrying out a census or survey or related activity pursuant to the provisions of title 13;

(5) to a recipient who has provided the agency with advance adequate written assurance that the record will be used solely as a statistical research or reporting record, and the record is to be transferred in a form that is not individually identifiable;

(6) to the National Archives and Records Administration as a record which has sufficient historical or other value to warrant its

continued preservation by the United States Government, or for evaluation by the Archivist of the United States or the designee of the Archivist to determine whether the record has such value;

(7) to another agency or to an instrumentality of any governmental jurisdiction within or under the control of the United States for a civil or criminal law enforcement activity if the activity is authorized by law, and if the head of the agency or instrumentality has made a written request to the agency which maintains the record specifying the particular portion desired and the law enforcement activity for which the record is sought;

(8) to a person pursuant to a showing of compelling circumstances affecting the health or safety of an individual if upon such disclosure notification is transmitted to the last known address of such individual;

(9) to either House of Congress, or, to the extent of matter within its jurisdiction, any committee or subcommittee thereof, any joint committee of Congress or subcommittee of any such joint committee;

(10) to the Comptroller General, or any of his authorized representatives, in the course of the performance of the duties of the General Accounting Office;

(11) pursuant to the order of a court of competent jurisdiction; or

(12) to a consumer reporting agency in accordance with section 3711(f) of title 31.

(c) Accounting of Certain Disclosures. - Each agency, with respect to each system of records under its control, shall -

(1) except for disclosures made under subsec-

tions (b)(1) or (b)(2) of this section, keep an accurate accounting of -

(A) the date, nature, and purpose of each disclosure of a record to any person or to another agency made under subsection (b) of this section; and

(B) the name and address of the person or agency to whom the disclosure is made;

(2) retain the accounting made under paragraph (1) of this subsection for at least five years or the life of the record, whichever is longer, after the disclosure for which the accounting is made;

(3) except for disclosures made under subsection (b)(7) of this section, make the accounting made under paragraph (1) of this subsection available to the individual named in the record at his request; and

(4) inform any person or other agency about any correction or notation of dispute made by the agency in accordance with subsection (d) of this section of any record that has been disclosed to the person or agency if an accounting of the disclosure was made.

(d) Access to Records. - Each agency that maintains a system of records shall -

(1) upon request by any individual to gain access to his record or to any information pertaining to him which is contained in the system, permit him and upon his request, a person of his own choosing to accompany him, to review the record and have a copy made of all or any portion thereof in a form comprehensible to him, except that the agency may require the individual to furnish a written statement authorizing discussion of that individual's record in the accompa-

nying person's presence;
(2) permit the individual to request amendment of a record pertaining to him and -
   (A) not later than 10 days (excluding Saturdays, Sundays, and legal public holidays) after the date of receipt of such request, acknowledge in writing such receipt; and
   (B) promptly, either -
      (i) make any correction of any portion thereof which the individual believes is not accurate, relevant, timely, or complete; or
      (ii) inform the individual of its refusal to amend the record in accordance with his request, the reason for the refusal, the procedures established by the agency for the individual to request a review of that refusal by the head of the agency or an officer designated by the head of the agency, and the name and business address of that official;
(3) permit the individual who disagrees with the refusal of the agency to amend his record to request a review of such refusal, and not later than 30 days (excluding Saturdays, Sundays, and legal public holidays) from the date on which the individual requests such review, complete such review and make a final determination unless, for good cause shown, the head of the agency extends such 30-day period; and if, after his review, the reviewing official also refuses to amend the record in accordance with the request, permit the individual to file with the agency a concise statement setting forth

the reasons for his disagreement with the refusal of the agency, and notify the individual of the provisions for judicial review of the reviewing official's determination under subsection (g)(1)(A) of this section;

(4) in any disclosure, containing information about which the individual has filed a statement of disagreement, occurring after the filing of the statement under paragraph (3) of this subsection, clearly note any portion of the record which is disputed and provide copies of the statement and, if the agency deems it appropriate, copies of a concise statement of the reasons of the agency for not making the amendments requested, to persons or other agencies to whom the disputed record has been disclosed; and

(5) nothing in this section shall allow an individual access to any information compiled in reasonable anticipation of a civil action or proceeding.

(e) Agency Requirements. - Each agency that maintains a system of records shall -

(1) maintain in its records only such information about an individual as is relevant and necessary to accomplish a purpose of the agency required to be accomplished by statute or by executive order of the President;

(2) collect information to the greatest extent practicable directly from the subject individual when the information may result in adverse determinations about an individual's rights, benefits, and privileges under Federal programs;

(3) inform each individual whom it asks to supply information, on the form which it uses

to collect the information or on a separate
form that can be retained by the individual -

(A) the authority (whether granted by
statute, or by executive order of the
President) which authorizes the solicitation of the information and whether
disclosure of such information is
mandatory or voluntary;

(B) the principal purpose or purposes for
which the information is intended to be
used;

(C) the routine uses which may be made of
the information, as published pursuant
to paragraph (4)(D) of this subsection;
and

(D) the effects on him, if any, of not providing all or any part of the requested
information;

(4) subject to the provisions of paragraph (11) of
this subsection, publish in the Federal
Register upon establishment or revision a
notice of the existence and character of the
system of records, which notice shall
include -

(A) the name and location of the system;

(B) the categories of individuals on whom
records are maintained in the system;

(C) the categories of records maintained in
the system;

(D) each routine use of the records contained in the system, including the categories of users and the purpose of such
use;

(E) the policies and practices of the agency
regarding storage, retrievability, access
controls, retention, and disposal of the
records;

(F)   the title and business address of the
agency official who is responsible for
the system of records;

(G)   the agency procedures whereby an individual can be notified at his request if
the system of records contains a record
pertaining to him;

(H)   the agency procedures whereby an individual can be notified at his request
how he can gain access to any record
pertaining to him contained in the system of records, and how he can contest
its content; and

(I)   the categories of sources of records in
the system;

(5)   maintain all records which are used by the
agency in making any determination about
any individual with such accuracy, rele-
vance, timeliness, and completeness as is
reasonably necessary to assure fairness to
the individual in the determination;

(6)   prior to disseminating any record about an
individual to any person other than an
agency, unless the dissemination is made
pursuant to subsection (b)(2) of this section,
make reasonable efforts to assure that such
records are accurate, complete, timely, and
relevant for agency purposes;

(7)   maintain no record describing how any individual exercises rights guaranteed by the
First Amendment unless expressly authorized by statute or by the individual about
whom the record is maintained or unless
pertinent to and within the scope of an
authorized law enforcement activity;

(8)   make reasonable efforts to serve notice on an
individual when any record on such indi-

vidual is made available to any person under compulsory legal process when such process becomes a matter of public record;

(9) establish rules of conduct for persons involved in the design, development, operation, or maintenance of any system of records, or in maintaining any record, and instruct each such person with respect to such rules and the requirements of this section, including any other rules and procedures adopted pursuant to this section and the penalties for noncompliance;

(10) establish appropriate administrative, technical, and physical safeguards to insure the security and confidentiality of records and to protect against any anticipated threats or hazards to their security or integrity which could result in substantial harm, embarrassment, inconvenience, or unfairness to any individual on whom information is maintained;

(11) at least 30 days prior to publication of information under paragraph (4)(D) of this subsection, publish in the Federal Register notice of any new use or intended use of the information in the system, and provide an opportunity for interested persons to submit written data, views, or arguments to the agency; and

(12) if such agency is a recipient agency or a source agency in a matching program with a non-Federal agency, with respect to any establishment or revision of a matching program, at least 30 days prior to conducting such program, publish in the Federal Register notice of such establishment or revision.

(f) Agency Rules. - In order to carry out the provisions of this section, each agency that maintains a system of records shall promulgate rules, in accordance with the requirements (including general notice) of section 553 of this title, which shall -

(1) establish procedures whereby an individual can be notified in response to his request if any system of records named by the individual contains a record pertaining to him;

(2) define reasonable times, places, and requirements for identifying an individual who requests his record or information pertaining to him before the agency shall make the record or information available to the individual;

(3) establish procedures for the disclosure to an individual upon his request of his record or information pertaining to him, including special procedure, if deemed necessary, for the disclosure to an individual of medical records, including psychological records, pertaining to him;

(4) establish procedures for reviewing a request from an individual concerning the amendment of any record or information pertaining to the individual, for making a determination on the request, for an appeal within the agency of an initial adverse agency determination, and for whatever additional means may be necessary for each individual to be able to exercise fully his rights under this section; and

(5) establish fees to be charged, if any, to any individual for making copies of his record, excluding the cost of any search for and review of the record.

The Office of the Federal Register shall biennially compile and publish the rules promulgated under this subsection and agency notices published under subsection (e)(4) of this section in a form available to the public at low cost.

(g)

    (1) Civil Remedies. - Whenever any agency

        (A) makes a determination under subsection (d)(3) of this section not to amend an individual's record in accordance with his request, or fails to make such review in conformity with that subsection;

        (B) refuses to comply with an individual request under subsection (d)(1) of this section;

        (C) fails to maintain any record concerning any individual with such accuracy, relevance, timeliness, and completeness as is necessary to assure fairness in any determination relating to the qualifications, character, rights, or opportunities of, or benefits to the individual that may be made on the basis of such record, and consequently a determination is made which is adverse to the individual; or

        (D) fails to comply with any other provision of this section, or any rule promulgated thereunder, in such a way as to have an adverse effect on an individual, the individual may bring a civil action against the agency, and the district courts of the United States shall have jurisdiction in the matters under the provisions of this subsection.

    (2)

        (A) In any suit brought under the provisions of subsection (g)(1)(A) of this section, the court may order the agency to amend the individual's record in accordance with his request or in such other way as the court may direct. In such a case the court shall determine the matter de novo.

(B) The court may assess against the United States reasonable attorney fees and other litigation costs reasonably incurred in any case under this paragraph in which the complainant has substantially prevailed.

(3)

(A) In any suit brought under the provisions of subsection (g)(1)(B) of this section, the court may enjoin the agency from withholding the records and order the production to the complainant of any agency records improperly withheld from him. In such a case the court shall determine the matter de novo, and may examine the contents of any agency records in camera to determine whether the records or any portion thereof may be withheld under any of the exemptions set forth in subsection (k) of this section, and the burden is on the agency to sustain its action.

(B) The court may assess against the United States reasonable attorney fees and other litigation costs reasonably incurred in any case under this paragraph in which the complainant has substantially prevailed.

(4) In any suit brought under the provisions of subsection (g)(1)(C) or (D) of this section in

which the court determines that the agency acted in a manner which was intentional or willful, the United States shall be liable to the individual in an amount equal to the sum of -

(A) actual damages sustained by the individual as a result of the refusal or failure, but in no case shall a person entitled to recovery receive less than the sum of $1,000; and

(B) the costs of the action together with reasonable attorney fees as determined by the court.

(5) An action to enforce any liability created under this section may be brought in the district court of the United States in the district in which the complainant resides, or has his principal place of business, or in which the agency records are situated, or in the District of Columbia, without regard to the amount in controversy, within two years from the date on which the cause of action arises, except that where an agency has materially and willfully misrepresented any information required under this section to be disclosed to an individual and the information so misrepresented is material to establishment of the liability of the agency to the individual under this section, the action may be brought at any time within two years after discovery by the individual of the misrepresentation. Nothing in this section shall be construed to authorize any civil action by reason of any injury sustained as the result of a disclosure of a record prior to September 27, 1975.

(h) Rights of Legal Guardians. - For the purposes of

this section, the parent of any minor, or the legal guardian of any individual who has been declared to be incompetent due to physical or mental incapacity or age by a court of competent jurisdiction, may act on behalf of the individual.

(i)(1) Criminal Penalties. - Any officer or employee of an agency, who by virtue of his employment or official position, has possession of, or access to, agency records which contain individually identifiable information the disclosure of which is prohibited by this section or by rules or regulations established thereunder, and who knowing that disclosure of the specific material is so prohibited, willfully discloses the material in any manner to any person or agency not entitled to receive it, shall be guilty of a misdemeanor and fined not more than $5,000.

(2) Any officer or employee of any agency who willfully maintains a system of records without meeting the notice requirements of subsection (e)(4) of this section shall be guilty of a misdemeanor and fined not more than $5,000.

(3) Any person who knowingly and willfully requests or obtains any record concerning an individual from an agency under false pretenses shall be guilty of a misdemeanor and fined not more than $5,000.

(j) General Exemptions. - The head of any agency may promulgate rules, in accordance with the requirements (including general notice) of sections 553(b)(1), (2), and (3), (c), and (e) of this title, to exempt any system of records within the agency from any part of this section except subsections (b), (c)(1) and (2), (e)(4)(A) through (F), (e)(6), (7), (9), (10), and

(11), and (i) if the system of records is -

(1)   maintained by the Central Intelligence Agency; or

(2)   maintained by an agency or component thereof which performs as its principal function any activity pertaining to the enforcement of criminal laws, including police efforts to prevent, control, or reduce crime or to apprehend criminals, and the activities of prosecutors, courts, correctional, probation, pardon, or parole authorities, and which consists of (A) information compiled for the purpose of identifying individual criminal offenders and alleged offenders and consisting only of identifying data and notations of arrests, the nature and disposition of criminal charges, sentencing, confinement, release, and parole and probation status; (B) information compiled for the purpose of a criminal investigation, including reports of informants and investigators, and associated with an identifiable individual; or (C) reports identifiable to an individual compiled at any stage of the process of enforcement of the criminal laws from arrest or indictment through release from supervision.

At the time rules are adopted under this subsection, the agency shall include in the statement required under section 553(c) of this title, the reasons why the system of records is to be exempted from a provision of this section.

(k)   Specific Exemptions. - The head of any agency may promulgate rules, in accordance with the requirements (including general notice) of sections 553(b)(1), (2), and (3), (c), and (e) of this title, to exempt any system of records within the agency from subsections (c)(3), (d), (e)(1), (e)(4)(G), (H), and (I) and (f) of this section if the system of records is -

(1) subject to the provisions of section 552(b)(1) of this title;

(2) investigatory material compiled for law enforcement purposes, other than material within the scope of subsection (j)(2) of this section: Provided, however, That if any individual is denied any right, privilege, or benefit that he would otherwise be entitled by Federal law, or for which he would otherwise be eligible, as a result of the maintenance of such material, such material shall be provided to such individual, except to the extent that the disclosure of such material would reveal the identity of a source who furnished information to the Government under an express promise that the identity of the source would be held in confidence, or, prior to the effective date of this section, under an implied promise that the identity of the source would be held in confidence;

(3) maintained in connection with providing protective services to the President of the United States or other individuals pursuant to section 3056 of title 18;

(4) required by statute to be maintained and used solely as statistical records;

(5) investigatory material compiled solely for the purpose of determining suitability, eligibility, or qualifications for Federal civilian employment, military service, Federal contracts, or access to classified information, but only to the extent that the disclosure of such material would reveal the identity of a source who furnished information to the Government

under an express promise that the identity of
the source would be held in confidence, or,
prior to the effective date of this section,
under an implied promise that the identity of
the source would be held in confidence;

(6) testing or examination material used solely
to determine individual qualifications for
appointment or promotion in the Federal
service the disclosure of which would com-
promise the objectivity or fairness of the
testing or examination process; or

(7) evaluation material used to determine
potential for promotion in the armed services, but only to the extent that the disclosure of such material would reveal the identity of a source who furnished information
to the Government under an express
promise that the identity of the source
would be held in confidence, or, prior to the
effective date of this section, under an
implied promise that the identity of the
source would be held in confidence.

At the time rules are adopted under this subsection, the
agency shall include in the statement required under section 553(c) of this title, the reasons why the system of
records is to be exempted from a provision of this section.

(l) Archival Records. - Each agency record which is
accepted by the Archivist of the United States for
storage, processing, and servicing in accordance
with section 3103 of title 44 shall, for the purposes of this section, be considered to be maintained by the agency which deposited the record
and shall be subject to the provisions of this section. The Archivist of the United States shall not
disclose the record except to the agency which
maintains the record, or under rules established

by that agency which are not inconsistent with the provisions of this section.

(2) Each agency record pertaining to an identifiable individual which was transferred to the National Archives of the United States as a record which has sufficient historical or other value to warrant its continued preservation by the United States Government, prior to the effective date of this section, shall, for the purposes of this section, be considered to be maintained by the National Archives and shall not be subject to the provisions of this section, except that a statement generally describing such records (modeled after the requirements relating to records subject to subsections (e)(4)(A) through (G) of this section) shall be published in the Federal Register.

(3) Each agency record pertaining to an identifiable individual which is transferred to the National Archives of the United States as a record which has sufficient historical or other value to warrant its continued preservation by the United States Government, on or after the effective date of this section, shall, for the purposes of this section, be considered to be maintained by the National Archives and shall be exempt from the requirements of this section except subsections (e)(4)(A) through (G) and (e)(9) of this section.

(m)

(1) Government Contractors. - When an agency provides by a contract for the operation by or on behalf of the agency of a system of records to accomplish an agency function, the agency shall, consistent with its authori-

ty, cause the requirements of this section to be applied to such system. For purposes of subsection (i) of this section any such contractor and any employee of such contractor, if such contract is agreed to on or after the effective date of this section, shall be considered to be an employee of an agency.

(2) A consumer reporting agency to which a record is disclosed under section 3711(f) of title 31 shall not be considered a contractor for the purposes of this section.

(n)   Mailing Lists. - An individual's name and address may not be sold or rented by an agency unless such action is specifically authorized by law. This provision shall not be construed to require the withholding of names and addresses otherwise permitted to be made public.

(o)   Matching Agreements. - (1) No record which is contained in a system of records may be disclosed to a recipient agency or non-Federal agency for use in a computer matching program except pursuant to a written agreement between the source agency and the recipient agency or non-Federal agency specifying -

  (A)   the purpose and legal authority for conducting the program;

  (B)   the justification for the program and the anticipated results, including a specific estimate of any savings;

  (C)   a description of the records that will be matched, including each data element that will be used, the approximate number of records that will be matched, and the projected starting and completion dates of the matching program;

  (D)   procedures for providing individualized notice at the time of application, and notice periodically thereafter as directed by the Data Integrity Board of such agency (subject to guidance provided by the Director of the Office of Management and Budget pursuant to subsection (v)), to -

   (i) applicants for and recipients of financial assistance or payments under Federal benefit programs, and

   (ii) applicants for and holders of positions as Federal personnel, that any information provided by such applicants, recipients, holders, and individuals may be subject to verification through matching programs;

(E) procedures for verifying information produced in such matching program as required by subsection (p);

(F) procedures for the retention and timely destruction of identifiable records created by a recipient agency or non-Federal agency in such matching program;

(G) procedures for ensuring the administrative, technical, and physical security of the records matched and the results of such programs;

(H) prohibitions on duplication and redisclosure of records provided by the source agency within or outside the recipient agency or the non-Federal agency, except where required by law or essential to the conduct of the matching program;

(I) procedures governing the use by a recipient agency or non-Federal agency of records provided in a matching program by a source agency, including procedures governing return of the records to the source agency or destruction of records used in such program;

(J)   information on assessments that have been made on the accuracy of the records that will be used in such matching program; and

(K) that the Comptroller General may have access to all records of a recipient agency or a non-Federal agency that the Comptroller General deems necessary in order to monitor or verify compliance with the agreement.

(2)

(A) A copy of each agreement entered into pursuant to paragraph (1) shall -

(i)   be transmitted to the Committee on Governmental Affairs of the Senate and the Committee on Government Operations of the House of Representatives; and

(ii) be available upon request to the public.

(B) No such agreement shall be effective until 30 days after the date on which such a copy is transmitted pursuant to subparagraph (A)(i).

(C) Such an agreement shall remain in effect only for such period, not to exceed 18 months, as the Data Integrity Board of the agency determines is appropriate in light of the purposes, and length of time necessary for the conduct, of the matching program.

(D) Within 3 months prior to the expiration of such an agreement pursuant to subparagraph (C), the Data Integrity Board of the agency may, without additional review, renew the matching agreement for a current, ongoing matching program for not more than one additional year if -

    (i)   such program will be conducted without any change; and

    (ii)   each party to the agreement certifies to the Board in writing that the program has been conducted in compliance with the agreement.

(p)   Verification and Opportunity to Contest Findings. - (1) In order to protect any individual whose records are used in a matching program, no recipient agency, non-Federal agency, or source agency may suspend, terminate, reduce, or make a final denial of any financial assistance or payment under a Federal benefit program to such individual, or take other adverse action against such individual, as a result of information produced by such matching program, until -

    (A)

        (i)   the agency has independently verified the information; or

        (ii)   the Data Integrity Board of the agency, or in the case of a non-Federal agency the Data Integrity Board of the source agency, determines in accordance with guidance issued by the Director of the Office of Management and Budget that -

           (I)   the information is limited to identification and amount of benefits paid by the source agency under a Federal benefit program; and

(II) there is a high degree of confidence that the information provided to the recipient agency is accurate;

(B) the individual receives a notice from the agency containing a statement of its findings and informing the individual of the opportunity to contest such findings; and

(C)

(i) the expiration of any time period established for the program by statute or regulation for the individual to respond to that notice; or

(ii) in the case of a program for which no such period is established, the end of the 30-day period beginning on the date on which notice under subparagraph (B) is mailed or otherwise provided to the individual.

(2) Independent verification referred to in paragraph (1) requires investigation and confirmation of specific information relating to an individual that is used as a basis for an adverse action against the individual, including where applicable investigation and confirmation of -

(A) the amount of any asset or income involved;

(B) whether such individual actually has or had access to such asset or income for such individual's own use; and

(C) the period or periods when the individual actually had such asset or income.

(3) Notwithstanding paragraph (1), an agency may take any appropriate action otherwise prohibited by such paragraph if the agency

determines that the public health or public
safety may be adversely affected or signifi-
cantly threatened during any notice period
required by such paragraph.

(q) Sanctions. -

(1) Notwithstanding any other provision of law,
no source agency may disclose any record
which is contained in a system of records to
a recipient agency or non-Federal agency for
a matching program if such source agency
has reason to believe that the requirements
of subsection (p), or any matching agreement entered into pursuant to subsection
(o), or both, are not being met by such recipient agency.

(2) No source agency may renew a matching
agreement unless -

(A) the recipient agency or non-Federal
agency has certified that it has com-
plied with the provisions of that agreement; and

(B) the source agency has no reason to believe
that the certification is inaccurate.

(r) Report on New Systems and Matching Programs.
- Each agency that proposes to establish or make
a significant change in a system of records or a
matching program shall provide adequate
advance notice of any such proposal (in dupli-
cate) to the Committee on Government
Operations of the House of Representatives, the
Committee on Governmental Affairs of the
Senate, and the Office of Management and
Budget in order to permit an evaluation of the
probable or potential effect of such proposal on
the privacy or other rights of individuals.

(s) Biennial Report. - The President shall biennially
submit to the Speaker of the House of

Representatives and the President pro tempore of the Senate a report -

(1) describing the actions of the Director of the Office of Management and Budget pursuant to section 6 of the Privacy Act of 1974 during the preceding 2 years;

(2) describing the exercise of individual rights of access and amendment under this section during such years;

(3) identifying changes in or additions to systems of records;

(4) containing such other information concerning administration of this section as may be necessary or useful to the Congress in reviewing the effectiveness of this section in carrying out the purposes of the Privacy Act of 1974.

(t) Effect of Other Laws. -

(1) No agency shall rely on any exemption contained in section 552 of this title to withhold from an individual any record which is otherwise accessible to such individual under the provisions of this section.

(2) No agency shall rely on any exemption in this section to withhold from an individual any record which is otherwise accessible to such individual under the provisions of section 552 of this title.

(u) Data Integrity Boards. -

(1) Every agency conducting or participating in a matching program shall establish a Data Integrity Board to oversee and coordinate among the various components of such agency the agency's implementation of this section.

(2) Each Data Integrity Board shall consist of senior officials designated by the head of the

agency, and shall include any senior official designated by the head of the agency as responsible for implementation of this section, and the inspector general of the agency, if any. The inspector general shall not serve as chairman of the Data Integrity Board.

(3)   Each Data Integrity Board -

(A)   shall review, approve, and maintain all written agreements for receipt or disclosure of agency records for matching programs to ensure compliance with subsection (o), and all relevant statutes, regulations, and guidelines;

(B)   shall review all matching programs in which the agency has participated during the year, either as a source agency or recipient agency, determine compliance with applicable laws, regulations, guidelines, and agency agreements, and assess the costs and benefits of such programs;

(C)   shall review all recurring matching programs in which the agency has participated during the year, either as a source agency or recipient agency, for continued justification for such disclosures;

(D)   shall compile an annual report, which shall be submitted to the head of the agency and the Office of Management and Budget and made available to the public on request, describing the matching activities of the agency, including -

(i)   matching programs in which the agency has participated as a source agency or recipient agency;

(ii)   matching agreements proposed under subsection (o) that were disapproved by the Board;

(iii) any changes in membership or structure of the Board in the preceding year;

(iv) the reasons for any waiver of the requirement in paragraph (4) of this section for completion and submission of a cost-benefit analysis prior to the approval of a matching program;

(v) any violations of matching agreements that have been alleged or identified and any corrective action taken; and

(vi) any other information required by the Director of the Office of Management and Budget to be included in such report;

(E) shall serve as a clearinghouse for receiving and providing information on the accuracy, completeness, and reliability of records used in matching programs;

(F) shall provide interpretation and guidance to agency components and personnel on the requirements of this section for matching programs;

(G) shall review agency recordkeeping and disposal policies and practices for matching programs to assure compliance with this section; and

(H) may review and report on any agency matching activities that are not matching programs.

(4)

(A) Except as provided in subparagraphs (B) and (C), a Data Integrity Board shall not approve any written agreement for a matching program unless the agency has completed and submitted to such Board a cost-benefit analysis of the proposed program and such analysis demonstrates that the program is likely to be cost effective. (FOOTNOTE 2: So in original. Probably should be 'cost-effective.')

(B) The Board may waive the requirements of subparagraph (A) of this paragraph if it determines in writing, in accordance with guidelines prescribed by the Director of the Office of Management and Budget, that a cost-benefit analysis is not required.

(C) A cost-benefit analysis shall not be required under subparagraph (A) prior to the initial approval of a written agreement for a matching program that is specifically required by statute. Any subsequent written agreement for such a program shall not be approved by the Data Integrity Board unless the agency has submitted a cost-benefit analysis of the program as conducted under the preceding approval of such agreement.

(5)

(A) If a matching agreement is disapproved by a Data Integrity Board, any party to such agreement may appeal the disapproval to the Director of the Office of Management and Budget. Timely notice of the filing of such an appeal shall be provided by the Director of the Office of Management and Budget to the Committee on Governmental Affairs of the Senate and the Committee on

Government Operations of the House of Representatives.

(B) The Director of the Office of Management and Budget may approve a matching agreement notwithstanding the disapproval of a Data Integrity Board if the Director determines that -

    (i)   the matching program will be consistent with all applicable legal, regulatory, and policy requirements;

    (ii) there is adequate evidence that the matching agreement will be cost-effective; and

    (iii) the matching program is in the public interest.

(C) The decision of the Director to approve a matching agreement shall not take effect until 30 days after it is reported to committees described in subparagraph (A).

(D) If the Data Integrity Board and the Director of the Office of Management and Budget disapprove a matching program proposed by the inspector general of an agency, the inspector general may report the disapproval to the head of the agency and to the Congress.

(6) The Director of the Office of Management and Budget shall, annually during the first 3 years after the date of enactment of this subsection and biennially thereafter, consolidate in a report to the Congress the information contained in the reports from the various Data Integrity Boards under paragraph (3)(D). Such report shall include detailed information about costs and benefits of

matching programs that are conducted during the period covered by such consolidated report, and shall identify each waiver granted by a Data Integrity Board of the requirement for completion and submission of a cost-benefit analysis and the reasons for granting the waiver.

(7) In the reports required by paragraphs (3)(D) and (6), agency matching activities that are not matching programs may be reported on an aggregate basis, if and to the extent necessary to protect ongoing law enforcement or counterintelligence investigations.

(v) Office of Management and Budget Responsibilities. - The Director of the Office of Management and Budget shall -

(1) develop and, after notice and opportunity for public comment, prescribe guidelines and regulations for the use of agencies in implementing the provisions of this section; and

(2) provide continuing assistance to and oversight of the implementation of this section by agencies.

(Added Pub. L. 93-579, Sec. 3, Dec. 31, 1974, 88 Stat. 1897, and amended Pub. L. 94-183, Sec. 2(2), Dec. 31, 1975, 89 Stat. 1057; Pub. L. 97-365, Sec. 2, Oct. 25, 1982, 96 Stat. 1749; Pub. L. 97-375, title II, Sec. 201(a), (b), Dec. 21, 1982, 96 Stat. 1821; Pub. L. 97-452, Sec. 2(a)(1), Jan. 12, 1983, 96 Stat. 2478; Pub. L. 98-477, Sec. 2(c), Oct. 15, 1984, 98 Stat. 2211; Pub. L. 98-497, title I, Sec. 107(g), Oct. 19, 1984, 98 Stat. 2292; Pub. L. 100-503, Sec. 2-6(a), 7, 8, Oct. 18, 1988, 102 Stat. 2507-2514; Pub. L. 101-508, title VII, Sec. 7201(b)(1), Nov. 5, 1990, 104 Stat. 1388-334.)

REFERENCES IN TEXT

Section 552(e) of this title, referred to in subsec. (a)(1), was redesignated section 552(f) of this title by section 1802(b) of Pub. L. 99-570.

Section 6103 of the Internal Revenue Code of 1986, referred to in subsec. (a)(8)(B)(iv), is classified to section 6103 of Title 26, Internal Revenue Code.

Sections 464 and 1137 of the Social Security Act, referred to in subsec. (a)(8)(B)(iv), are classified to sections 664 and 1320b-7, respectively, of Title 42, The Public Health and Welfare.

For effective date of this section, referred to in subsecs. (k)(2), (5), (7), (l)(2), (3), and (m), see Effective Date note below.

Section 6 of the Privacy Act of 1974, referred to in subsec. (s)(1), is section 6 of Pub. L. 93-579, which was set out below and was repealed by section 6(c) of Pub. L. 100-503. For classification of the Privacy Act of 1974, referred to in subsec. (s)(4), see Short Title note below.

The date of enactment of this subsection, referred to in subsec. (u)(6), is the date of enactment of Pub. L. 100-503 which enacted subsec. (u) of this section, and which was approved Oct. 18, 1988.

CODIFICATION
Section 552a of former Title 5, Executive Departments and Government Officers and Employees, was transferred to section 2244 of Title 7, Agriculture.

AMENDMENTS
1990 - Subsec. (p). Pub. L. 101-508 amended subsec. (p) generally, restating former pars. (1) and (3) as par. (1), adding provisions relating to Data Integrity Boards, and restating former pars. (2) and (4) as (2) and (3), respectively.

1988 - Subsec. (a)(8) to (13). Pub. L. 100-503, Sec. 5, added pars. (8) to (13).

Subsec. (e)(12). Pub. L. 100-503, Sec. 3(a), added par. (12).

Subsec. (f). Pub. L. 100-503, Sec. 7, substituted 'biennially' for 'annually' in last sentence.
Subsecs. (o) to (q). Pub. L. 100-503, Sec. 2(2), added subsecs. (o) to (q). Former subsecs. (o) to (q) redesignated (r) to (t), respectively.

Subsec. (r). Pub. L. 100-503, Sec. 3(b), inserted 'and matching programs' in heading and amended text generally. Prior to amendment, text read as follows: 'Each agency shall provide adequate advance notice to Congress and the Office of Management and Budget of any proposal to establish or alter any system of records in order to permit an evaluation of the probable or potential effect of such proposal on the privacy and other personal or property rights of individuals or the disclosure of information relating to such individuals, and its effect on the preservation of the constitutional principles of federalism and separation of powers.'

Pub. L. 100-503, Sec. 2(1), redesignated former subsec. (o) as (r).

Subsec. (s). Pub. L. 100-503, Sec. 8, substituted 'Biennial' for 'Annual' in heading, 'biennially submit' for 'annually submit' in introductory provisions, 'preceding 2 years' for 'preceding year' in par. (1), and 'such years' for 'such year' in par. (2).

Pub. L. 100-503, Sec. 2(1), redesignated former subsec. (p) as (s).
Subsec. (t). Pub. L. 100-503, Sec. 2(1), redesignated former subsec. (q) as (t).

Subsec. (u). Pub. L. 100-503, Sec. 4, added subsec. (u).

Subsec. (v). Pub. L. 100-503, Sec. 6(a), added subsec. (v).

1984 - Subsec. (b)(6). Pub. L. 98-497, Sec. 107(g)(1), substituted 'National Archives and Records Administration' for 'National Archives of the United States', and 'Archivist of the United States or the designee of the Archivist' for 'Administrator of General Services or his designee'.

Subsec. (l)(1). Pub. L. 98-497, Sec. 107(g)(2), substituted 'Archivist of the United States' for 'Administrator of General Services' in two places.

Subsec. (q). Pub. L. 98-477 designated existing provisions as par. (1) and added par. (2).

1983 - Subsec. (b)(12). Pub. L. 97-452 substituted 'section 3711(f) of title 31' for 'section 3(d) of the Federal Claims Collection Act of 1966 (31 U.S.C. 952(d))'.

Subsec. (m)(2). Pub. L. 97-452 substituted 'section 3711(f) of title 31' for 'section 3(d) of the Federal Claims Collection Act of 1966 (31 U.S.C. 952(d))'.

1982 - Subsec. (b)(12). Pub. L. 97-365, Sec. 2(a), added par. (12).
Subsec. (e)(4). Pub. L. 97-375, Sec. 201(a), substituted 'upon establishment or revision' for 'at least annually' after 'Federal Register'.

Subsec. (m). Pub. L. 97-365, Sec. 2(b), designated existing provisions as par. (1) and added par. (2).
Subsec. (p). Pub. L. 97-375, Sec. 201(b), substituted provisions requiring annual submission of a report by the President to the Speaker of the House and President pro

tempore of the Senate relating to the Director of the Office of Management and Budget, individual rights of access, changes or additions to systems of records, and other necessary or useful information, for provisions which had directed the President to submit to the Speaker of the House and the President of the Senate, by June 30 of each calendar year, a consolidated report, separately listing for each Federal agency the number of records contained in any system of records which were exempted from the application of this section under the provisions of subsections (j) and (k) of this section during the preceding calendar year, and the reasons for the exemptions, and such other information as indicate efforts to administer fully this section.

1975 - Subsec. (g)(5). Pub. L. 94-183 substituted 'to September 27, 1975' for 'to the effective date of this section'.

EFFECTIVE DATE OF 1988 AMENDMENT
Section 10 of Pub. L. 100-503, as amended by Pub. L. 101-56, Sec. 2, July 19, 1989, 103 Stat. 149, provided that:
> '(a) In General. - Except as provided in subsections (b) and (c), the amendments made by this Act (amending this section and repealing provisions set out as a note below) shall take effect 9 months after the date of enactment of this Act (Oct. 18, 1988).
> '(b) Exceptions. - The amendment made by sections 3(b), 6, 7, and 8 of this Act (amending this section and repealing provisions set out as a note below) shall take effect upon enactment.
> '(c) Effective Date Delayed for Existing Programs. - In the case of any matching program (as defined in section 552a(a)(8) of title 5, United States Code, as added by section 5 of this Act) in operation before June 1, 1989, the amendments made by

this Act (other than the amendments described in subsection (b)) shall take effect January 1, 1990, if -

'(1) such matching program is identified by an agency as being in operation before June 1, 1989; and

'(2) such identification is -

'(A) submitted by the agency to the Committee on Governmental Affairs of the Senate, the Committee on Government Operations of the House of Representatives, and the Office of Management and Budget before August 1, 1989, in a report which contains a schedule showing the dates on which the agency expects to have such matching program in compliance with the amendments made by this Act, and

'(B) published by the Office of Management and Budget in the Federal Register, before September 15, 1989.'

EFFECTIVE DATE OF 1984 AMENDMENT
Amendment by Pub. L. 98-497 effective Apr. 1, 1985, see section 301 of Pub. L. 98-497, set out as a note under section 2102 of Title 44, Public Printing and Documents.

EFFECTIVE DATE
Section 8 of Pub. L. 93-579 provided that: 'The provisions of this Act (enacting this section and provisions set out as notes under this section) shall be effective on and after the date of enactment (Dec. 31, 1974), except that the amendments made by sections 3 and 4 (enacting this section and amending analysis preceding section 500 of this title) shall become effective 270 days following the day on which this Act is enacted.'

SHORT TITLE OF 1990 AMENDMENT
Section 7201(a) of Pub. L. 101-508 provided that: 'This section (amending this section and enacting provisions set out as notes below) may be cited as the 'Computer Matching and Privacy Protection Amendments of 1990'.'

SHORT TITLE OF 1989 AMENDMENT
Pub. L. 101-56, Sec. 1, July 19, 1989, 103 Stat. 149, provided that: 'This Act (amending section 10 of Pub. L. 100-503, set out as a note above) may be cited as the 'Computer Matching and Privacy Protection Act Amendments of 1989'.'

SHORT TITLE OF 1988 AMENDMENT
Section 1 of Pub. L. 100-503 provided that: 'This Act (amending this section, enacting provisions set out as notes above and below, and repealing provisions set out as a note below) may be cited as the 'Computer Matching and Privacy Protection Act of 1988'.'

SHORT TITLE
Section 1 of Pub. L. 93-579 provided: 'That this Act (enacting this section and provisions set out as notes under this section) may be cited as the 'Privacy Act of 1974'.'

DELEGATION OF FUNCTIONS
Functions of Director of Office of Management and Budget under this section delegated to Administrator for Office of Information and Regulatory Affairs by section 3 of Pub. L. 96-511, Dec. 11, 1980, 94 Stat. 2825, set out as a note under section 3503 of Title 44, Public Printing and Documents.

PUBLICATION OF GUIDANCE UNDER SUBSECTION (P)(1)(A)(II)
Section 7201(b)(2) of Pub. L. 101-508 provided that: 'Not

later than 90 days after the date of the enactment of this Act (Nov. 5, 1990), the Director of the Office of Management and Budget shall publish guidance under subsection (p)(1)(A)(ii) of section 552a of title 5, United States Code, as amended by this Act.'

LIMITATION ON APPLICATION OF VERIFICATION REQUIREMENT

Section 7201(c) of Pub. L. 101-508 provided that: 'Section 552a(p)(1)(A)(ii)(II) of title 5, United States Code, as amended by section 2 (probably means section 7201(b)(1) of Pub. L. 101-508), shall not apply to a program referred to in paragraph (1), (2), or (4) of section 1137(b) of the Social Security Act (42 U.S.C. 1320b-7), until the earlier of -

'(1) the date on which the Data Integrity Board of the Federal agency which administers that program determines that there is not a high degree of confidence that information provided by that agency under Federal matching programs is accurate; or

'(2) 30 days after the date of publication of guidance under section 2(b) (probably means section 7201(b)(2) of Pub. L. 101-508, set out as a note above).'

EFFECTIVE DATE DELAYED FOR CERTAIN EDUCATION BENEFITS COMPUTER MATCHING PROGRAMS

Pub. L. 101-366, title II, Sec. 206(d), Aug. 15, 1990, 104 Stat. 442, provided that:

'(1) In the case of computer matching programs between the Department of Veterans Affairs and the Department of Defense in the administration of education benefits programs under chapters 30 and 32 of title 38 and chapter 106 of title 10, United States Code, the amendments made to section 552a of title

5, United States Code, by the Computer
Matching and Privacy Protection Act of 1988
(Pub. L. 100-503) (other than the amendments
made by section 10(b) of that Act) (see
Effective Date of 1988 Amendment note
above) shall take effect on October 1, 1990.
'(2) For purposes of this subsection, the term
'matching program' has the same meaning
provided in section 552a(a)(8) of title 5,
United States Code.'

IMPLEMENTATION GUIDANCE FOR 1988 AMENDMENTS
Section 6(b) of Pub. L. 100-503 provided that: 'The
Director shall, pursuant to section 552a(v) of title 5,
United States Code, develop guidelines and regulations
for the use of agencies in implementing the amendments
made by this Act (amending this section and repealing
provisions set out as a note below) not later than 8 months
after the date of enactment of this Act (Oct. 18, 1988).'

CONSTRUCTION OF 1988 AMENDMENTS
Section 9 of Pub. L. 100-503 provided that: 'Nothing
in the amendments made by this Act (amending this section and repealing provisions set out as a note below) shall
be construed to authorize -
'(1) the establishment or maintenance by any
agency of a national data bank that com-
bines, merges, or links information on individuals maintained in systems of records by
other Federal agencies;
'(2) the direct linking of computerized systems of
records maintained by Federal agencies;
'(3) the computer matching of records not otherwise authorized by law; or
'(4) the disclosure of records for computer
matching except to a Federal, State, or local
agency.'

CONGRESSIONAL FINDINGS AND
STATEMENT OF PURPOSE

Section 2 of Pub. L. 93-579 provided that:

'(a) The Congress finds that -

'(1) the privacy of an individual is directly affected by the collection, maintenance, use, and dissemination of personal information by Federal agencies;

'(2) the increasing use of computers and sophisticated information technology, while essential to the efficient operations of the Government, has greatly magnified the harm to individual privacy that can occur from any collection, maintenance, use, or dissemination of personal information;

'(3) the opportunities for an individual to secure employment, insurance, and credit, and his right to due process, and other legal protections are endangered by the misuse of certain information systems;

'(4) the right to privacy is a personal and fundamental right protected by the Constitution of the United States; and

'(5) in order to protect the privacy of individuals identified in information systems maintained by Federal agencies, it is necessary and proper for the Congress to regulate the collection, maintenance, use, and dissemination of information by such agencies.

'(b) The purpose of this Act (enacting this section and provisions set out as notes under this section) is to provide certain safeguards for an individual against an invasion of personal privacy by requiring Federal agencies, except as otherwise provided by law, to -

'(1) permit an individual to determine what records pertaining to him are collected, maintained, used, or disseminated by such agencies;

'(2) permit an individual to prevent records pertaining to him obtained by such agencies for a particular purpose from being used or made available for another purpose without his consent;

'(3) permit an individual to gain access to information pertaining to him in Federal agency records, to have a copy made of all or any portion thereof, and to correct or amend such records;

'(4) collect, maintain, use, or disseminate any record of identifiable personal information in a manner that assures that such action is for a necessary and lawful purpose, that the information is current and accurate for its intended use, and that adequate safeguards are provided to prevent misuse of such information;

'(5) permit exemptions from the requirements with respect to records provided in this Act only in those cases where there is an important public policy need for such exemption as has been determined by specific statutory authority; and '(6) be subject to civil suit for any damages which occur as a result of willful or intentional action which violates any individual's rights under this Act.'

PRIVACY PROTECTION STUDY COMMISSION
Section 5 of Pub. L. 93-579, as amended by Pub. L. 95-38, June 1, 1977, 91 Stat. 179, which established the Privacy Protection Study Commission and provided that the Commission study data banks, automated data processing programs and information systems of governmental, regional and private organizations to determine standards and

procedures in force for protection of personal information, that the Commission report to the President and Congress the extent to which requirements and principles of section 552a of title 5 should be applied to the information practices of those organizations, and that it make other legislative recommendations to protect the privacy of individuals while meeting the legitimate informational needs of government and society, ceased to exist on September 30, 1977, pursuant to section 5(g) of Pub. L. 93-579.

GUIDELINES AND REGULATIONS FOR MAINTENANCE OF PRIVACY AND PROTECTION OF RECORDS OF INDIVIDUALS

Section 6 of Pub. L. 93-579, which provided that the Office of Management and Budget shall develop guidelines and regulations for use of agencies in implementing provisions of this section and provide continuing assistance to and oversight of the implementation of the provisions of such section by agencies, was repealed by Pub. L. 100-503, Sec. 6(c), Oct. 18, 1988, 102 Stat. 2513.

DISCLOSURE OF SOCIAL SECURITY NUMBER

Section 7 of Pub. L. 93-579 provided that:
'(a)
(1) It shall be unlawful for any Federal, State or local government agency to deny to any individual any right, benefit, or privilege provided by law because of such individual's refusal to disclose his social security account number.

'(2) the (The) provisions of paragraph (1) of this subsection shall not apply with respect to -
'(A) any disclosure which is required by Federal statute, or '(B) the disclosure of a social security number to any Federal, State, or local agency maintaining a system of records in existence and operat-

ing before January 1, 1975, if such disclosure was required under statute or regulation adopted prior to such date to verify the identity of an individual.

'(b) Any Federal, State, or local government agency which requests an individual to disclose his social security account number shall inform that individual whether that disclosure is mandatory or voluntary, by what statutory or other authority such number is solicited, and what uses will be made of it.'

AUTHORIZATION OF APPROPRIATIONS TO PRIVACY PROTECTION STUDY COMMISSION

Section 9 of Pub. L. 93-579, as amended by Pub. L. 94-394, Sept. 3, 1976, 90 Stat. 1198, authorized appropriations for the period beginning July 1, 1975, and ending on September 30, 1977.

SECTION REFERRED TO IN OTHER SECTIONS

This section is referred to in sections 552b, 1212, 3111, 7133 of this title; title 7 sections 1359hh, 1359ii, 2204b; title 10 sections 424, 1102; title 12 section 1715z; title 15 section 278g-3; title 16 sections 410cc-35, 1536; title 20 sections 1080a, 1221e-1; title 26 sections 6103, 7852; title 31 sections 3701, 3711, 3718, 3729, 3733; title 38 sections 1784A, 3301; title 39 section 410; title 42 sections 300aa-25, 402, 405, 1306, 9660; title 44 sections 2906, 3501, 3504; title 46 sections 7702, 9303.

18 USC S. 2710

S. 2710. Wrongful disclosure of video tape rental or sale records

APPENDIX E

THE VIDEO PRIVACY PROTECTION ACT (BORK BILL) (AS OF APRIL 1993)

(a) Definitions. For purposes of this section—
  (1) the term "consumer" means any renter, purchaser, or subscriber of goods or services from a video tape service provider;
  (2) the term "ordinary course of business" means only debt collection activities, order fulfillment, request processing, and the transfer of ownership;
  (3) the term "personally identifiable information" includes information which identifies a person as having requested or obtained specific video materials or services from a video tape service provider; and
  (4) the term "video tape service provider" means any person, engaged in the business, in or affecting interstate or foreign com-

merce, of rental, sale, or delivery of prere-
corded video cassette tapes or similar audio
visual materials, or any person or other entity to whom a disclosure is made under subparagraph (D) or (E) of subsection (b)(2), but
only with respect to the information contained in the disclosure.

(b) Video tape rental and sale records.

    (1) A video tape service provider who knowing-
ly discloses, to any person, personally identifiable information concerning any consumer of such provider shall be liable to the
aggrieved person for the relief provided in
subsection (d).

    (2) A video tape service provider may disclose
personally identifiable information concerning any consumer—

      (A) to the consumer;

      (B) to any person with the informed, writ-
ten consent of the consumer given at
the time the disclosure is sought;

      (C) to a law enforcement agency pursuant to
a warrant issued under the Federal
Rules of Criminal Procedure, an equivalent State warrant, a grand jury subpoe-
na, or a court order;

      (D) to any person if the disclosure is solely
of the names and addresses of con-
sumers and if—

        (i) the video tape service provider has
provided the consumer with the
opportunity, in a clear and conspicuous manner, to prohibit such
disclosure; and

        (ii) the disclosure does not identify the

title, description, or subject matter of any video tapes or other audio visual material; however, the subject matter of such materials may be disclosed if the disclosure is for the exclusive use of marketing goods and services directly to the consumer;

(E) to any person if the disclosure is incident to the ordinary course of business of the video tape service provider; or

(F) pursuant to a court order, in a civil proceeding upon a showing of compelling need for the information that cannot be accommodated by any other means, if—

(i) the consumer is given reasonable notice, by the person seeking the disclosure, of the court proceeding relevant to the issuance of the court order; and

(ii) the consumer is afforded the opportunity to appear and contest the claim of the person seeking the disclosure.

If an order is granted pursuant to subparagraph (C) or (F), the court shall impose appropriate safeguards against unauthorized disclosure.

(3) Court orders authorizing disclosure under subparagraph (C) shall issue only with prior notice to the consumer and only if the law enforcement agency shows that there is probable cause to believe that the records or other information sought are relevant to a legitimate law enforcement inquiry. In the case of a State

government authority, such a court order shall not issue if prohibited by the law of such State. A court issuing an order pursuant to this section, on a motion made promptly by the video tape service provider, may quash or modify such order if the information or records requested are unreasonably voluminous in nature or if compliance with such order otherwise would cause an unreasonable burden on such provider.

(c) Civil action.

    (1) Any person aggrieved by any act of a person in violation of this section may bring a civil action in a United States district court.

    (2) The court may award—

        (A) actual damages but not less than liquidated damages in an amount of $2,500;

        (B) punitive damages;

        (C) reasonable attorneys' fees and other litigation costs reasonably incurred; and

        (D) such other preliminary and equitable relief as the court determines to be appropriate.

    (3) No action may be brought under this subsection unless such action is begun within 2 years from the date of the act complained of or the date of discovery.

    (4) No liability shall result from lawful disclosure permitted by this section.

(d) Personally identifiable information. Personally identifiable information obtained in any manner other than as provided in this section shall not be received in evidence in any trial, hearing, arbitration, or other proceeding in or before any court, grand jury, department, officer, agency, regulatory body, legislative committee, or other authority of the United States, a State, or a political subdivision of a State.

(e) Destruction of old records. A person subject to this section shall destroy personally identifiable information as soon as practicable, but no later than one year from the date the information is no longer necessary for the purpose for which it was collected and there are no pending requests or orders for access to such information under subsection (b)(2) or (c)(2) or pursuant to a court order.

(f) Preemption. The provisions of this section preempt only the provisions of State or local law that require disclosure prohibited by this section.

BIBLIOGRAPHY

Bacard, Andre. *The Computer Privacy Handbook.* Peachpit Press, 1995.

Black, Henry Campbell. *M.A. Black's Law Dictionary*, 6th Ed. West Publishing, 1990.

Bulzomi, Michael J., J.D. "The Workplace Privacy of Law Enforcement and Public Employees." *FBI Law Enforcement Bulletin.* (June 1998): 27.

Coates, James. "Tribune Business News," *Chicago Tribune.* (May 23, 1993).

Consumer Reports. "Are You a Target for Identity Theft?" (September 1997): 10.

Fuljenz, Michael. "What to Do if You're Stopped by the Police." *American Survival Guide* (March 1998): 58.

Gillmor, Dan. "Privacy on the Information Super-Highway: How to Maintain It." *Detroit Free Press.* Internet at: ftp.msen.com (May 1, 1994).

Givens, Beth. *The Privacy Rights Handbook.* New York: Avon Books, 1997.

Hammond, Bob. *Super Privacy.* Boulder, Colo.: Paladin Press, 1997.

Kaysing, Bill. *Privacy: How to Get It. How to Enjoy It.* Fountain Valley, Cal.: Eden Press, 1977.

Luger, Jack. *How to Use Mail Drops for Profit, Privacy, and Self-Protection.* Port Townsend, Wash.: Loompanics Unlimited, 1996.

Marshall, Patrick G. "Your Right to Privacy." *Editorial Research Reports.* (January 20, 1989): 30.

Maxwell, David A. *Private Security Law: Case Studies.* Newton, Mass.: Butterworth-Heinemann, 1993.

McClellan, Grant S. *The Right to Privacy.* Bronx, New York: H.W. Wilson Co., 1976.

McWhirter, Darien A. *Search, Seizure, and Privacy.* Phoenix, Ariz.: The Oryx Press, 1994.

Party, Boston T. *Bulletproof Privacy: How to Live Hidden, Happy, and Free!* Durango, Colo.: Javelin Press, 1997.

Pate, James L. "Outrage." *Soldier of Fortune.* (June 1998): 48.

Pietrantoni, M. "Cell Phones and Privacy." *American Survival Guide.* (July 1998): 14.

Quittner, Joshua. "No Privacy on the Web." *Time* (June 2, 1997): 64.

Rothfeder, Jeffrey. *Privacy for Sale.* New York: Simon & Schuster, 1992.

Scott, Gini Graham. *Mind Your Own Business: The Battle for Personal Privacy.* Insight Books, 1995.

Shannon, M.L. *The Bug Book: Wireless Microphones and Surveillance Transmitters.* San Francisco: Lysias Press, 1993.

_____. *Digital Privacy: A Guide to Computer Security.* Boulder, Colo.: Paladin Press, 1993.

Spinello, Richard A. "The End of Privacy." *America.* (January 4, 1997): 9.

Stallings, William. *Protect Your Privacy: A Guide for PGP Users.* New York: Prentice Hall, 1995.

Whigham-Desir, Marjorie. "Protect Your Identity." *Black Enterprise.* (March 1997): 98.

ABOUT THE AUTHOR

Michael E. Chesbro is a senior counterintelligence special agent with the U.S. Department of Defense, focusing on security in the special operations environment. He holds a bachelor of science in security management from St. John's University, is a certified independent paralegal, and is professionally certified as a protection officer and security supervisor from the International Foundation for Protection Officers. He is a board-certified forensic examiner with the American College of Forensic Examiners and a diplomate of the American Board of Forensic Examiners and the American Board of Law Enforcement Experts.

As a life-long advocate of individual sovereignty and Constitutional freedoms, Chesbro has watched with growing concern as individual rights have been eroded and guaranteed freedoms have been trampled by government agen-

171

cies and organizations in the name of "policy" or to meet somebody's political agenda.

Like all government officials, Chesbro has taken a solemn oath to preserve, protect, and defend the Constitution of the United States. He believes that an oath is a life-long commitment that cannot be set aside in the name of policy or politic. Through his writings and his organization, the Citizens Law Enforcement Research and Investigations Committee (CLERIC), Chesbro seeks to defend our rights and freedoms, believing that if we "enlighten the people generally, tyranny and oppression of body and mind will vanish like evil spirits at the dawn of day."